Father to Daughter

Father to Daughter

The Family Letters of Maxwell Perkins

Edited by
Bertha Perkins Frothingham, Louise Perkins King,
and Ruth King Porter

Andrews and McMeel
A Universal Press Syndicate Company
Kansas City

Library of Congress Catalog Card Number: 95-60237

ISBN: 0-8362-0487-5

Originally printed by Empty Bowl, Port Townsend, Washington.

Book and jacket design by Glenn Suokko, Woodstock, Vermont.

To Zippy, Jane, and Nancy,
who are so much missed by Bert and Peggy

Bertha Perkins.
WINDSOR.
Vermont
NEW YORK
N.Y.
U.S. POSTAGE
Paint

NEW YORK
AUG 25
9 30 PM
1920
N.Y.
U.S. POSTAGE
E
C/o Mrs. M. E. Perkins.
Windsor.
Vermont.

NEW YORK
JUL 27
U.S. POSTAGE
Bertha Perkins
Windsor
Vermont
C/o Mrs M. E. Perkins

Contents

Introduction

My father, Maxwell Perkins, became a distinguished editor, and is now sometimes referred to as legendary. To me, his eldest daughter, he was simply the center of all our lives. As a young child in Plainfield, New Jersey, I would stop playing with my sisters every evening, and go down with my current book to sit on the stone wall in front of our house. There I would have a good view up the street, and when I saw him walking up from the train I would run to him and we would walk back together. I would be deeply content.

Our father grew up in Plainfield, New Jersey, and in the summers in Windsor, Vermont. His grandfather William Maxwell Evarts, who had twelve children, had bought six houses in a row down Main Street in Windsor, and many acres of land and woods behind them. There was a large pond and the woods called "Paradise" by the family, and on the other side of the Connecticut River, Cornish, New Hampshire, where Augustus St. Gaudens lived and worked, along with many other creative artists.

My father was the second of three boys, all very close in age, followed by two daughters and finally by Louis, the fourth son and sixth child. The three older boys roamed all over the fields and woods with their Evarts cousins. These summers were so wonderful that our father later made sure his five children would spend their summers there too, and learn to love Windsor as he did. This was quite a sacrifice on his part because he was left alone in New York, coming up by train only every second week, for the weekend. During those lonely weeks in the city he wrote to our mother and to one child in turn, each day. It was our mother, Louise, who gathered the letters up and saved them. After his death in 1947, she and his secretary, Irma Muench, went through them and returned them to the daughters to whom they had been written.

We were five girls and he dearly loved us all, though he sometimes thought wistfully of how nice it would be to have a son who would be interested in wars and the rough games that boys would understand. We tried to please him, but Nancy made the mistake of wearing high heels when he took her to Gettysburg, much shortening their tramp over the battlefield, and when he read *War and Peace* aloud, we all sighed with relief when we got to the "peace part," as opposed to the "war part" he loved.

We all had nicknames, which were used by both our parents more often than our given names. We were Bertha, Berta, Bert; Elizabeth, E, Lisbet, and finally Zippy, which stuck; Louise, Peggy, Peggotty, Pegs; Jane, Jenny, Jen; Nancy, Nance. We grew up at first in Plainfield, New Jersey, and then in New Canaan, Connecticut, where we moved in 1924. Nancy, who was born in 1925, never knew Plainfield.

As these family letters show, Max Perkins was interested in all his children and guided and encouraged us without ever seeming to do so. It was not until I read *Editor to Author* for the first time, after his death, that I realized that he brought out the very best in his writers in exactly the same way that he had encouraged us to do the very best we were capable of. John Hall Wheelock, in his introduction to *Editor to Author*, says, "the recognizing, the encouraging, the guiding of talent—this, in his opinion, was a sacred task worth any amount of effort, of risk, of time expended." He put the same time and effort into encouraging and guiding his daughters, each one according to her particular interests and talents.

The other thing we shared with his writers was his silent

but unmistakable respect for our feelings. Jane once told me of an incident that happened in Cornish, a few miles outside Windsor, where we were spending the summer. Zippy had just received her driver's license and had permission to take the car and drive over to Windsor alone. It was an important step for her into the grown-up world. Jane, still only a little girl, and our father were saying good-bye to her in the driveway when Jane said, "Can I go too?" Zippy's face fell. Jane, hurt and seeing that she was not wanted, said no more, and the car drove off. "Daddy was very nice to me all that day," Jane told me. He was aware of how Zippy felt, aware of how Jane felt; and though he never said a word, Jane felt his understanding and sympathy so deeply that she never forgot it.

Marcia Davenport speaks of this wonderful way of communicating without words when she says, "He gave us infinite, tolerant understanding," and later she tells of long silences, when they met at the Ritz before his train, and says, "I would go home, feeling both calm and exhilarated, and next morning my problems would have disappeared."

By never preparing us ahead of time or explaining afterwards, he helped us feel the whole impact of a new experience. When I was about seven, I was enthralled by Howard Pyle's stories of the knights of the Round Table, which my father had brought home to me, of course. I was not interested in the ladies, who did little more than drop scarves out of windows, but saw myself as a knight on a great charger, in full armor, with a sword at my side and lance in my hand. One Saturday afternoon in Plainfield, my father and I went for our usual cross-country walk, this time up a steep hill through the woods. Suddenly we emerged into a clearing and looked down on a valley, in the center of which stood a castle—a real castle with battlements and turrets and everything a castle should have. He said nothing, and for a long time I couldn't say anything either. When I finally recovered enough to demand an explanation, he only smiled and said it was time to go home. He never explained, and he never would take me back. Time and reality have never had a chance to dim the thrill of that magic moment for me.

Another time I remember, when I was six, opening my eyes on a hot midsummer morning in Plainfield to see my father peeking around the door. He was dressed for the office, but when he saw I was awake, he picked me up, very quietly, so as not to wake the other two children, and took me into his room, next to Mother's. There was a bassinet I had never seen before, and in it a crying baby, waving tiny hands and feet. Again, he said nothing, but I, looking down on it, said, "I don't know who it is or what it is." He took me back to my bed in the nursery and left me there to wonder and dream until someone came to get us up, saying brightly, "You have a baby sister."

At the time these letters were written, between 1915 and 1929, Max Perkins was a young man starting out on a new career, with a growing family and a young wife who was a creative writer herself and who shared his interest in books. He was very lucky, and well aware of it, because he was working for Charles Scribner's Sons, who stood for and believed in the very things he did. His long friendships with Charles Scribner and John Hall Wheelock, and his secretary Irma Wyckoff Muench, were only beginning to develop into the team that worked so well for so long. "Nothing is as important as a book can be," he once wrote in a letter to Thomas Wolfe. His life came to be dedicated to that precept. His office was his second home, or possibly his first home, since he spent many more accumulated hours there than anywhere else in the course of his life. He would no more have left Scribners than he would have deserted his wife and children.

Father to Daughter

Though these letters often speak of how much he hated the hot, steamy city, he really loved it too. He was born in New York but moved to Plainfield when he was very young. After he graduated from Harvard in 1907, he went to New York and got a job on *The New York Times*. He was excited about the city and says in one of his letters that, in those days, he "couldn't get enough of it." Working for the *Times* and taking long walks for exercise, a life-long habit, he grew to know the city intimately.

Years later in the '30s, when the older girls had left home, he and Mother and Jane and Nancy lived for a few years at 246 East 49th Street. Jane used to tell of how he would come home early from the office on Saturdays, and she and Nancy would go with him all over the city. They went to Chinatown, and to Staten Island on the ferry, passing the Statue of Liberty, crossed the great bridges to Brooklyn and Queens, and took the subway to Columbia and the Palisades. The two girls looked forward to these trips all week.

As we got older, he stopped illustrating his letters to us. Apparently, pictures were for children only, though we didn't see why. By the time we were married, the telephone had come into its own, and he called us frequently. He was very busy by then, and letters from him were typewritten and rather formal. Four of us lived nearby anyway, and he delighted in our children, five of whom were boys, and one of them a Max. Only Peg lived far away in Ohio.

Though the letters had stopped, every now and then a book would come from Scribners. They were beautifully packed, and it took a bit of work to release them. Inside would be a card saying, "Compliments of Charles Scribner's Sons." It was a joy, especially in the dark days of the war, to get these new books, which he had edited, and plunge into them: books like *The Yearling, The Valley of Decision, The His-*

tory of *Rome Hanks and Kindred Matters,* and *Of Time and the River,* with its moving dedication to him.

Letter writing seems to have been an easy and natural way for our father to express himself. He dictated thousands of business letters to Irma Muench, some of which eloquently express his feelings about censorship and freedom of speech, as well as about writing. Many of these letters were published in *Editor to Author.* He also wrote many letters over the years to his dear friend Elizabeth Lemmon, and sometimes this was his only outlet during the hardest years of his life. Scott Berg has quoted from these letters extensively in *Max Perkins, Editor of Genius.*

We hope these family letters will show our father as a vigorous young man starting out on a new and intensely interesting career, with no idea where it might take him. On another level, they are simply the tender and perceptive letters of a father to his children.

Bertha Perkins Frothingham
Windsor, Vermont

Some Memories by Peggy

I know a story about my father that reveals clearly how he felt about books. My mother told me that when she and he went to someone's house (very seldom, as he hated to go out!), he would stand in front of the bookcase, looking the books over. My mother said the people they were visiting always became nervous and awkward because they thought that he was judging them by the books they owned. But, as my mother said, nothing could have been further from the truth! He thought that reading was pleasure; one should read what one likes to read; there's no right or wrong to it. My father was simply looking for old friends in the bookcase!

It's surprising when we had so wonderful an upbringing, that we did so little with it. I have always felt, with pain, that we were a disappointment to him, all of us. "A man who does not marry is a coward," he said, "and a woman who does is a coward." He meant that the man avoids responsibility, but a woman falls into marriage as a soft, easy solution to her life. I don't think it's true any longer but it was then, and that's exactly what we did, all five of us; we flopped safely into marriage. He would have liked a daughter who was an adventurer, a vagabond, and he certainly wanted a daughter (better than nothing!) in the World War. He always regretted that he was not sent overseas in the First World War. At first, it seems strange that so gentle a man loved war, but I think there were two reasons for this. One, for his generation, war was still gallantry, courage and adventure, and two, so many great books come out of war. War certainly has a literary side to it.

Here is a memory that shows the lightness of his humor and his tenderness. In the middle of a deep pond we used to swim in there was a rock rising up to about two feet below the surface. My father said that anyone who could swim out to the rock had definitely learned to swim. I remember my father and one of my sisters standing on the rock when I started from shore to swim out. I thrashed and splashed and choked and just as I got near, I sank. My father pulled me up. My sister cried, "She still can't swim because she went under." My father said, "Oh no, she was just looking for the rock." I remember how we three stood there, clinging to each other because the rock was slippery, and laughing!

He was very fastidious. My parents were invited to a dinner party given by a famous beauty. In those days, women's dresses were cut very low in back. When they came home we asked, "Is she really beautiful?" He got a look of disgust on his face. We said, "You don't mean she's ugly?" He said scornfully, "The marks of her daytime clothes were on her back." Poor woman! Another time he was invited to meet Wendell Wilkie and he came home very angry with Wilkie because he had snubbed his own wife in front of everyone.

He did know poverty, his own brand of poverty. He once said, "You girls don't know what it is to be poor! When I was a reporter, I lived in one small room with only a cold water tap down the hall." "But, Daddy," we said, "what did you do when you wanted a bath?" "Oh," he said, "I went to the Harvard Club."

When I remember him as an old man, (but he was only 62 when he died!) sad and worn and disappointed, I try to look further back and remind myself how he went to the operetta "Babes in Toyland" over and over, more than ten times I think. There must have been something in it that matched that lovely, light, teasing gaiety that was in him when he was young.

Father to Daughter

I hope these anecdotes reveal a little of my father. Of course, anyone who wants to learn more should read Scott Berg's *Editor of Genius,* or better still, *Editor to Author,* the collection of his letters to many writers.

Louise Perkins King
Marion, Massachusetts

Acknowledgments

Our Mother had a huge wooden chest in a room in the basement of the New Canaan house, which she called the "store room." Somehow all, or almost all, letters received by the family eventually found their way into this chest. It was far from being a well-organized filing system, but it did preserve them safely.

After our father's death in 1947, and after his wonderfully efficient secretary, Mrs. Osmer Muench, still affectionately known to all of us as Miss Wyckoff, had put all his affairs in order at the office, and retired from Scribners, she came to New Canaan to help Mother deal with the contents of the big chest.

Miss Wyckoff was fascinated by all the letters to the children and urged us to get them published. She knew about the valentines he had made for us when we were very young, because she had often been asked to type the verses but, of course, had never seen the letters. She showed them to Mr. Charles Scribner III, who said that it would be difficult and expensive to reproduce them, as indeed it would have been at that time. Modern technology has made it much easier for us to reproduce them now, but how sorry we are that Miss Wyckoff is not here to see them.

Peggy started things moving in 1989 when she had her eighty-four letters copied and then turned the originals over to the Houghton Library at Harvard. This inspired me (Bert) to do something about mine. Because I am the eldest, I had even more letters than she did.

When my daughter Jane was about sixteen, she had spent her spring vacation putting my letters in chronological order and between plastic sheets. They had to be taken out to be copied. We found they were very fragile and difficult to work with. When it was done, I sent for Jane's and Zippy's letters and copied them too. Zippy had quite a few letters; Jane had seven, and only one letter and a poem to Nancy have survived. Our father very carefully wrote to each child in turn, so we can not explain why the numbers are so uneven.

This was as far as I had planned to go, but when they were all copied and the handwriting transcribed and I read them all over together, I realized how very charming they are, and, above all, how they show a side of my father's character unknown to his business associates or to his biographer. It seemed that the time had come to publish the book Miss Wyckoff had wanted so much to see.

We wish we could have included all the letters, but to keep this book from being too long, we had to leave out almost a third of them. In selecting these letters, we tried to choose those that showed our father's special interest and concern for each individual child and to always include those that referred to his work.

It was difficult to put them in chronological order because he headed his letters with the day, possibly the month, and rarely the year. We often had to guess at the year by figuring out where we were living and the age of the child he was writing to. Most of these letters were illustrated. We tried to arrange the drawings as they were originally. In some cases drawings were deleted for reasons of space, but we have been careful never to alter the text in any way, even to correct it. (Our father was a very poor speller, and his punctuation was even worse.)

We wish to express our thanks to the friends who helped us so much with this project: to Priscilla Whitcomb who was the first to transcribe the original letters, and who did so with great patience and skill and unfailing interest; to Brita Bergland for her work in clarifying and copying the drawings and text; to Mark Pendergrast for his interest; to Scott Berg for his enthusiasm and encouragement; to Erika Gaffney who was enormously helpful in selecting the letters and who seemed to have an unerring sense of just how the letters should be arranged; to David Godine for his good suggestions; to Jerry Gorsline for his expert advice and assistance; and to Glenn Suokko, the designer whose magic touch transformed our manuscript into what it is now.

Bertha Perkins Frothingham
Windsor, Vermont, January 1995

Chronology

June 1907	Max Perkins graduated from Harvard
1908–1909	Worked for *The New York Times*
Spring 1910	Joined Charles Scribner's Sons as advertising manager
December 1910	Married Louise Saunders
1914	Moved to Scribners editorial department
July 1916	Went to the Mexican border with the U.S. Cavalry Reserves during the Mexican War
Summer 1920	Scribners published *This Side of Paradise*, by F. Scott Fitzgerald, edited by Max Perkins
Fall 1924	The Perkinses moved from Plainfield, New Jersey, to New Canaan, Connecticut
October 1925	Scribners published *The Knave of Hearts*, by Louise Saunders Perkins
Fall 1926	Scribners published *The Sun Also Rises*, by Ernest Hemingway, edited by Max Perkins
Spring 1927	Max and Louise Perkins traveled to London, England

Father to Daughter

January – *March 1928*	Bert's trip to Europe
March 1929	The end of the letters in this book
October 1929	Scribners published *Look Homeward, Angel*, by Thomas Wolfe, edited by Max Perkins
1933 – 1939	The Perkinses lived in New York in the Saunders' house at 246 East 49th Street
Spring 1935	Louise Perkins took Zippy and Peggy to Europe
Spring 1938	Scribners published *The Yearling*, by Marjorie Kinnan Rawlings, edited by Max Perkins
Spring 1940	Jane Perkins graduated from Vassar
1940 – 1945	Jane first worked as an editor, then left to work for British Information Services, as part of the war effort
1945 – 1948	Jane worked as an editor for William Sloane Associates

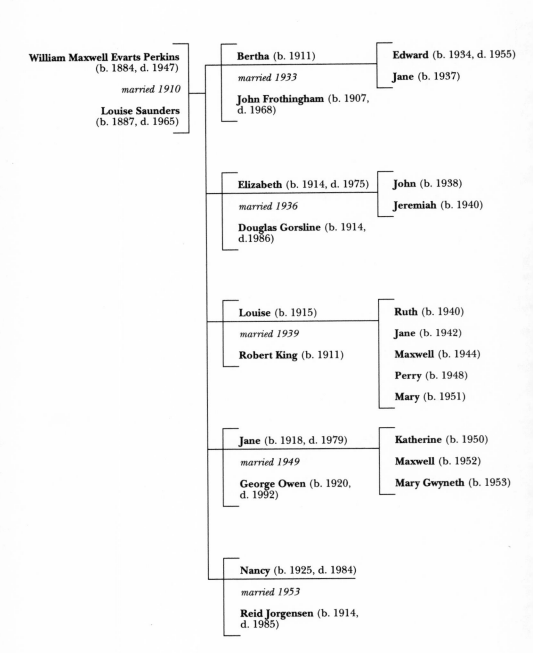

Father to Daughter

Max Perkins at about seventeen and Louise Saunders at twenty.

Max, in the middle, on the Mexican border
with the National Guard.

Father to Daughter

Left:
Louise Perkins with
Peggy, Bert, and Zippy.

Below:
Bert, age 3, in
Windsor with Louise.

The New Canaan house in the 1920's.

Father to Daughter

Jane, Zippy, Bert, and Peggy, about 1922.

Nancy, age 12, in a dress designed and made by Peggy, 1938.

The Perkins' house in the 1920's.

The pond in the 1920's.

Father to Daughter

*The pond with Mt. Ascutney in the background from a pastel
by Donna Maria DeCreeft. (Photo by Frank Lather)*

Paradise in the 1920's.

Max Perkins in the 1930's.

Father to Daughter

Father to Daughter
The Family Letters of Maxwell Perkins

THE WALK

Dear Bert:—

I went for a walk today, and the funniest things happened.
First I came to the bridge where you and I always go and
stopped to look at the ducks.

They were splashing in the water and putting their
heads under, and when they saw me they said; quack, quack,
quack as if they were angry. I said: What's the matter? aren't
you glad to see me Mrs. Ducks; and they all said, "not without Bertha." And they came out of the water and walked
after me up the road.

Father to Daughter

Then we came to the fuzzy little white dog that always barked at you and Daddy on the hill. He barked and barked! This bark said — "Where's Bertha? Where's Bertha? Go- and get- Bertha"! and he would not be quiet, and followed daddy and the Ducks.

Pretty soon, at the top of the hill a big grey rabbit with a fluffy tail popped out of the bushes and got right in Daddy's way. He seemed to want to talk so Daddy sat down on a stump, and then he said: — "You always bring Bertha on Sunday, and I came to see her go bye. Now where is she? Go and get her."

The Walk

Then the Bunny followed too and the dog and the ducks, all saying "quack quack, Bow wow, and squeak, squeak, wheres Bertha? Go and get her!"

Well, we got to the top of the mountain and came to the little pond that you used to throw stones into; and once when you threw a stone in the Snake came out. While we stood there Daddy suddenly heard "Hiss"! hiss! And there was Mr. Snake! He kept saying "You go right home and get Bertha!"

Daddy saw there was only one thing to do: he sat down on the ground and said, Bertha had to go to Windsor to get pink cheeks and to be with Mother and Lisbeth. But I miss her just as much as you all, Mr. Snake, and Mr. Rabbit and Mr. Dog, and Misses Ducks; and when she comes back I shall bring her right up to see you, honest! And they all said "Will you promise" and I said, "I promise." And then they all said, "Give her my love when you write," and scampered, or flew, or wriggled off home.

Father to Daughter

[1915]

Berta darlin:—

You have a little baby cousin, much littler than Ruth. He has a pinkey red face and a red nose no bigger than your thumb, and his eyes are all squeezed up tight like a baby kittys and he has no hair on his head at all. He lies on his back but can turn over himself, and he cries most of the time, but just for fun. He has no name. What do you think Auntie Jean ought to name him?

Daddy

The Walk

O my Bertha, Were you seasick on the boat when Daddy was
so far away and couldn't come to you? You were never sick
before but Daddy saw you and carried you up and down; —
before there was a Peggy, or even a Lisbeth, — before you
can remember, you were so little. And this time I didn't even
know my little girl *was* sick. That makes me feel so sorry. But
you had fun didn't you, on the boat? Will you write me all
about it?

THE BORDER

Our father enlisted in the New Jersey National Guard in 1915, and in 1916 Squadron A was sent down to guard the Mexican border. They were there two months and, in spite of being very homesick for his family, it was a wonderful experience for him, and the only time he ever crossed the continent.

Dear Bertha: — Daddy has to camp out again tonight, — to sleep in his clothes, on the ground, rolled up in a blanket.

Father to Daughter

Then, tomorrow, he has to shoot a gun all day — you have to shut one eye when you shoot a gun. First, you shoot kneeling, then lying, then sitting.

I hope he will be able to hit something.

Then he packs up for Bacation.

Daddy

Monday, July 2

Berta darlin: — All the soldiers you saw in camp, and
daddy, and the horses and
the cooking stoves, are now
on a train going to "the border." And they will be going
on the train for five days and
nights all the time. Then
they will get out of the train
and take out the horses and
put up their tents again and
live the way you saw them in
camp.

We are going on the
train still Berta, through the
prairies, — great big fields as
far as you can see, and no houses or people, but ever so
many cows and bulls and Jack Rabbits with very long hind
legs and ears. They can run as fast as a horse and jump over
a fence. The soldiers whistle at them to make them do it.

We did pass five cow-girls on horses and waved to them,
and pretty soon we all looked out, and here came one of
them making her horse run and run till she was right up by
the train; and we all cheered and she lifted her whip above
her head and waved it. Wasn't she a good horse rider?

Whenever this train goes through a town all the people
come out and stand by the track and wave flags and hand-
kerchiefs and cheer, and the soldiers lean out the windows
and wave their hats and cheer back. And some are very

Father to Daughter

happy because they think they are going to war. But those that have three little girls and their mother at home are very sorry and hope they will get many letters from them and will not be forgotten.

Your father
Love to Lisbeth and Peggy

Here we are riding across the desert.

August 5

Berta my darlin, Wouldn't it be funny if two days a week mother took every single thing, beds and all, out of the house and put them in the street. Thats what we do with our tents. Then they look like this.

Then we pour water on the floor and stamp on it and rake it, and put all our things back again. The sun has made them all nice and clean, — at least it is supposed to.

The first thing we know in the morning a man blows a trumpet and that means time to get up. Then I call to the men in our tent, "All up." And as we do not undress to go to bed we are soon all ready; and then Uncle Brown calls "fall in" and we run out of our tents and stand in a long line, like in the picture. And he calls each name, and when he calls "Corporal Perkins" I call out "here"; and thats what every man does when his name is called. Then we go up and give the horses a drink before we have our breakfast. And now so many men are sick that we often lead three horses at one time, like in this picture.

Father to Daughter

Then we have to give the horses exercise so they won't get sick: — We ride on one horse and lead another. That takes a long time, — till lunch time; and after lunch we sit down and write to our little girls and their mothers.

Father

August 8

Berta darlin, There are snakes here, called rattle snakes because they have rattles fastened to their tales; and when you come near one of them they rattle, so you know it and go away before they hurt you. Did mother tell you about the man in our tent who was so afraid of snakes? Well, you know

snakes Hiss! and just after he had been talking about them in the tent at night when we were all in bed in the dark there was a Hiss! and then another long "hiss"! and the man was so frightened. And it wasn't a snake at all: only another man blowing into his air pillow with his breath to fill it with air. Wasn't that funny?

Then about jumping on a train: I was riding out in the desert on a fast horse and along came a train going to New York; and I thought I could just ride this horse up beside that train and jump off the horse onto the train, and it would take me to my Berta and Lisbeth and Peggy. But that would be wrong. Daddys and Mothers have to do things they dont want to do all the time just like children do; and Daddy has to stay here because it would not be right to go home yet.

Bert, we had inspection of tents today, and Daddys tent, the officers said, was very neat and well arranged — Mother would think that funny. In my tent we fasten everything we can to our beds, — our guns, and spurs and lariats, and canteens for water, and everything we can; then we never lose anything. Daddys tent is near the end just the way it was at Seagirt when you came down. I wish you could only come here the way you did then and I would show you where it is. I never see any little girls here but one soldiers little girl named Emily. She lives at a hotel all the time and looks like this, — Shes about seven, and I would have told her about you if I had not heard so many other soldiers tell her that they had "little girls like her at home" that I thought she might be tired of it.

Your own
"Father"

Father to Daughter

August 24

Berta darlin: —

You would have laughed if you had seen our troop marching this morning: A mule led us, a brown mule with long
ears. It was the funniest thing. A mule is like a big donkey,
and he is always up to mischief. Some people think mules
can laugh. They are always playing jokes on other mules and
on people, just as this brown mule did on us. He ran away
from his driver and came out on the field where we were
drilling and stood beside the Captain. No one could make
him go away. And when the Captain told us to march, Mr.
Mule marched in front of us and no matter where we went
Mr. Mule marched away just as fast, ahead. All the way home

he led us and all the other soldiers in the camp thought it was the best joke. They all laughed. Everyone laughs at mules.

Bert, this is a very short letter, but I am writing it outdoors near a light soldiers are using to build a platform by — and most of these soldiers I don't know — and they all come and look at my pictures and laugh and ask about them and I tell them they are for my own little girl. But I dont like to have the strange soldiers see my letter to my little girl, and so I must stop.

Your own
Father

Father to Daughter

Berta my darlin, If you dressed up like a soldier and came down here we would ride together like this.

On Sundays we would go on a pic nic; ride out to the mountains, tie up our horses and eat lunch. What fun we would have.

And at night we would go home to bed in *our* tent. But I think the guns and things would be too big for you, Berta darlin. Will you go on pic nics with me when I get home?

Thank you for sending me the alphabet. It was a very good alphabet I thought. And I'm so glad you are going to send me more letters. I love to get them. Wasn't Lisbeth cunning to say when Daddy came home she would sing "Goodbye Mammie, Daddys gone away." She is a little joker: I put a kiss for her inside this letter.

"Father"

Berta Darlin: — A funny thing happened to me last night: I was Corporal of the Guard again; And I went out in the dark with a lantern to look at the horses; And I was walking along quietly like this — It was very dark —; and all of a

sudden — bang! — I was at the bottom of a deep hole in the ground the soldiers has dug to put a water pipe in. I had a hard time climbing out; — but I wasn't hurt.

Then we had a terrible thunder storm; the rain was so thick that it was dark; and the wind blew harder than it ever blows in Plainfield: it blew some tents away; and the lightening flashed so bright that you had to shut your eyes.

Late in the night when you and Mother and Lisbeth and all were asleep I sat on the ground, in the dark, on a rubber coat and thought about you all. Did it make you dream about me?

"Father"

"Father"

Father to Daughter

Berta darlin: This is a cowboy leading his horse. You see he is *really* a man, or else a very *big* boy. I am glad you are teaching Lisbeth her colors, and Peggy to say words: I would think you will make a *very* good teacher.

Berta, I cut off my moustache because it felt so stiff and sticky in this hot place and my hair has grown a good deal. So I look more like I used to look before we came to the border.

This is a picture of daddys cot as it looks now. All the soldiers have these cots: they are comfortable.

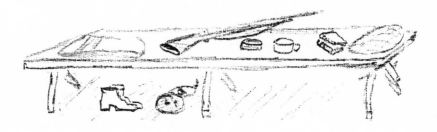

Yesterday one mans bed caught afire from the flame of a lantern, and we thought the whole tent would burn up, — it was full of flames, and the man was burned. But we put that fire out just the way Mother put out the fire on your dress, — by pressing a blanket against it.

Then we had what you call a Sandstorm. Sand flew through the air on the wind, like rain, — only more of it than ever of rain — and you couldnt see, and it hurt your face. And all the tents shook and *almost* fell down. And one blew right away in the air, — that was the tent you saw that they cook in. And Berta, it blew away one soldiers trousers, — he had hung them out to dry — and they were the only ones he had.

You must kiss Lisbeth, and tell her I sent the kiss to you to give her in the envelope; and kiss Peggy and tell her so too. But Mother will know without telling her.

I love to get your letters.

Father

Soldiers Playing Cards

Father to Daughter

Father to Daughter

SUMMERS
IN WINDSOR

New Jersey summers are very hot, and it was a probably a good idea to move the family to a more comfortable place for the summer. But it was hardly necessary to send us on an eight- or nine-hour trip to Vermont. Our mother would have been very happy at Sea Girt, New Jersey, where her family often went when she was young. But it was entirely our father's idea. Windsor was in his blood, and he wanted his children to know and love it the way he did.

Windsor was a wonderful place, and still is, and we all loved it. Our grandmother had a large red brick house on Main Street— one of the six houses that had belonged to her father. Behind them was "The Pond," and behind that "Paradise," and overlooking it all, serene and beautiful Mount Ascutney; "Old Mother Ascutney," our father called it. We rented one house or another every summer, sometimes in Cornish, New Hampshire, across the Connecticut River, but wherever we were we spent our days in or near the pond with the many cousins who had also come for the summer. When our father came up for Saturday and Sunday every other week, he would take us for long walks up the mountain or over the hills, gather the cousins together for games, and swim always. On Sunday night he would rush down to the station, barely catch his train, and be gone. Until he came back, the letters would come, always with pictures.

Louis Perkins, our father's youngest brother, was wounded in action in World War I. He was much younger than his brother, Max, who had tried to take the place of his father, who had died when Louis was very young. Max used to write illustrated letters to Louis, too, when he was a boy; unfortunately those letters have not survived.

Father to Daughter

July 23, [1918]

Dear Bert: —

This is me crying because YOU HAVE GONE AWAY AND HAVE NOT WRITTEN ME A LETTER. IF YOU WRITE I *WONT* CRY.

UNCLE LOUIS IS IN THE BIG BATTLE NOW BEATING THE GERMANS AND MAKING THEM RUN AWAY FAST AS THEY CAN. YOU MUST PRAY HARD HE WONT BE HURT: HE IS – MY – BEST – BROTHER AND YOUR – BEST – UNCLE

I HAD – A – GOOD – SWIM – TODAY. I – HOPE YOU –
WILL – HAVE – ONE – TOMORROW

LOVE – TO – AUNT – JEAN

Zippy had three imaginary friends: Mincey-Boo, Ploplakes and Pucherly. Both her parents were fascinated by these friends and Mother wrote several children's stories about them.

Dear Elizabeth: — Didnt this letter s'prise you? It is a normous letter for a teeny weeny girl to get. I think it is the normousest letter ever written, — except perhaps some letters from Kings. I could never have written it if some friends of yours hadn't helped me — Ploplakes, Mincey-Boo and Pucherly. Mincey is a pretty little fairy girl with gold eyes. She jumped on my shoulders and pulled my hair and said, tell Lisbeth I sent her the dream about the young little boy in the policemans suit and whenever she is specially good and kind I will send her other nice dreams.

Ploplakes is a fat little boy in many colored clothes with a tassel on his cap. He stood on the desk and said "I like Lisbeth best when shes jolly and full of fun because that is the way I am and so everybody likes me and when she is that way I promise everyone will love her always." But Pucherly is mischievous and he danced on the back of my chair and said "I like to tease Lisbeth, she is so funny so sometimes I make noises at night to frighten her a little, ha! ha! But really, I take care of her and would let nothing hurt her. Then all three Pucherly, Ploplakes and Mincey-Boo laughed like tinkle-bells and vanished! I jumped up and looked every-

where but I could not find them. I suppose they went back to you to take care of you while you were asleep.

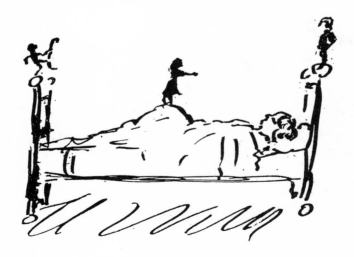

Father to Daughter

Lisbeth, in New York the streets are covered with asphalt which is stuff that gets soft and sticky when it is hot; and if it got just a little bit softer and stickier people would stick fast to them like flys to flypaper. Wouldn't that be funny. The policeman would have to come and pull them out.

Lisbet, when Mother is quite well, let's all go on a pic-nic and take supper and cook it, like this:

Daddy

Darlin Bertha: —

Did you know there were lots of little girls in New York who never saw a hop-toad or a bully cow or even *grass?*

I saw ever so many of them in the station, some almost as little as Lisbeth, and they all had bags: a kind lady was taking them out of the city to see birds and trees and brooks for the first time on a pic nic. They were all chattering, — as happy and excited as if they were going to Christmas. Isn't that funny! All they had ever seen was houses and streets and wagons and people, — not even trees.

Once Daddy took some of these poor little girls into the country with some other people, and they loved it. But one little girl was so excited and played so hard that she got sick and Daddy had to carry her. But she soon got well.

Daddy.

Father to Daughter

"Bopa" was what we called our mother's father. Our father stayed at Bopa's house in New York during the summers. Bopa was a mining engineer and had been all over the world, as he was an authority on compressed air. His wife died when our mother was sixteen and her sister was twelve. He often took one daughter or the other on his business trips, but they didn't enjoy it much because he was so busy and they were often lonely.

Mother told of how she and he went to Mexico City one time, and he told her to stay in the hotel room as it wouldn't be safe for her to go out alone. Mother, who loved people and was fascinated by what she saw from her window, started talking in broken Spanish to the men in the street who were selling baskets and trinkets to the tourists. Then she had an idea: she let down a basket from her window on a string with some money in it. They filled it with their wares, then she drew it up and let it down again with more money in it. When Bopa came back, the room was full of souvenirs and Mother had had a lovely afternoon.

Summers in Windsor

Monday, September 10th

Darling Peg:
Have mother put you in a trunk, with your blanket, so you can curl up and go to sleep. You can lie on a pillow.

Then get her to check the trunk to Bopa's apartment and put in a baggage car at the station.

Your Daddy

　　　　　　　　　　　　　　　Father to Daughter

Dearest E: —

Tell me how everything is in Windsor: is Pasture Hill still there, and Mt. Ascutney? Take a walk everyday so you will be ready to climb Ascutney with Bert and me. I am coming up Friday night, on the regular train. Today I stood a long time in line and bought my ticket. Can you tell in the picture which one is I?

I went to see an actress today. She told me of a little boy younger than you who was in a play; and one thing this boy had to do was pretend to cry near the stage but not on it. That was part of the play. And once there was a visitor where the child was when the play was going on; and he didn't know what the child was to do. So when the child cried he was fooled — he thought it was real and that the child was spoiling the play; — so he caught the child and clapped his hand over his mouth; and this scared him so he really did cry. Isn't that funny? Wasn't the child a good actor to fool him?

Daddy

Father to Daughter

August 22nd

Darling Berta: — Mother and I and Wee Beastie are lonely
without our little girls, — Wee Beastie is the loneliest because he doesn't know where you have gone and what fun
you will have on the sand & in the water. You must all get
brown from the sun and Lisbeth must get ten new freckles
everyday.

Did you and Lisbeth change your clothes after I went
away? or did you go off in my coats looking as you did this
morning? That would have been funny. How the conductor
would have laughed!

Mother has gone up to see Jane. I wonder if she knows
her three big sisters are away. I'm going to get Minthy-Boo
to come and teach me the Baby language so I can talk to her
now you and Peggy and Lisbeth can't talk to me. I'm sure
the fairies know the baby language if they will only tell it.

Goodby darling
Daddy

Talking To Jane

Dear Peg: — This is Uncle Tommy and I having breakfast after a sleepless night on a Sleeper.

This is you and I swimming out to the float in the pond.

Father to Daughter

And this is you writing a letter to your Daddy.

I wish you were here tonight for Bopa is away and you could sleep in his bed. I would take care of you.

Daddy

On our walks up Pasture Hill, there was a rock which had broken so that the top piece was like a lid. Our father said it was a wishing stone, and if you lifted up the top and whispered a wish into it, the wish would come true.

One time Zippy wished for a horse, and Bert, as usual, for a suit of armor. Later, as we rested on top of the hill, we saw two horses grazing in the distance.

"There you are, Zip," he said, "There's your horse. All you have to do is go and get him."

Zippy wasn't at all sure, and the horses were awfully far away. "Oh Daddy, don't be silly. And, anyway, what about Bert's armor?"

"It's on the back of the other horse," he said.

It was very frustrating. We were pretty sure he was teasing us, but maybe we should have gone. We were such cowards.

Father to Daughter

Back to the city again, Bertha!
I'm back in the city again;
O I'm trying to feel that I like a club meal
For I'm back in the city again.

And in this gloomy old club again too. And it seems as if it were still last summer, and that you had all been away for ever so long. I know you were very tired before you got to Windsor for I was by the end of the afternoon. Bert, I went to sleep in the barber's shop while he was cutting my hair. Wont E think that is funny?

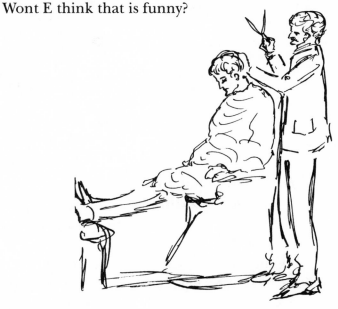

Bert, I had dinner with a daddy who said the men played baseball where his family were; but he was afraid to play because then his son would laugh at him, he plays so badly. I said, "all my daughters laugh at me and sing a song about my being afraid of a cow."

Tell mother to try to get me a section on the night train on Monday.

Your Daddy

Darling E: A funny thing happened. I came to Plainfield to chop wood, got into my khaki clothes and started across the fields where the cows are. As I passed one of them I heard a

deep, gruff, voice-like sound. It sounded like a song, — like "Polly, Wolly, doodle all day." I looked at the cow hard and there was no sound. But when I turned around it began again, — a very deep voice sang:

"Bertha Perkins is afraid of a cow   and then:
"Sing Polly, Wolly, doodle all day"   *Elizabeth Perkins is afraid of a cow*
                                       Sing Polly Wolly doodle all day

I pretended I was going on and then, suddenly turned round again: — it was the cow! She sang it again and winked. — So you see what comes of making fun of your daddy.

I saw Edwin too and he showed me the young chickins. They are doing very well.

When I was chopping wood I heard a rustle in a nearby bush. I went over to it and there was Brownie playing he was an Indian. While I was resting he talked to me and I told him how Bert jumped into the brook. He asked if you did and I said you couldn't because you were on my shoulders.

Daddy

Dear Peg:

Do you see me in the picture going to the hotel. There I am with my bag; and I have time to write to you before I go to my office. When I got on the train last night I thought at first I would have to stay up all night, for they had sold the bed I was to have. But I got another. I woke up once and thought Lisbeth was crying and that that man who likes to stay awake all night to pull her hair was at it again; — but it was only the car wheels squeaking. This is the way you sleep in the train — one above another.

Bert and I know what we can do to keep that man from pulling Lisbet's hair and not spoil his fun: I'll bring up the big doll on Friday: Then we'll make up Lisbet's bed with a pillow at each end and put Lisbet's head at the foot and the doll's head where Lisbet's used to be. Then the man will pull the Doll's hair all night and *he* will be happy; and Lisbet will sleep all night and she will be happy.

Like this

Tonight I will to write Bert and tomorrow Lisbeth.

Daddy

Dearest Bert: — This is the way we do at this gloomy old

club. Doesn't it seem silly? I got into a party like this. I had to sit and sit a long time wishing I could go and write to you and mother. A man (the one who was afraid to have his boy see him play ball) just asked me to dinner. I told him I wasn't hungry enough because we didn't reach New York till ten, and then had breakfast; — and so I had lunch late too. I had a berth right over Walter; and I was the first one up, and got all dressed; and then waked him.

Well, we had fun on Pasture hill, didn't we? — Even if you did fall into the brook. I'll draw a picture of you in the brook.

Your Daddy

Father to Daughter

Monday, July 14th, 1919

Dearest Peg: —

Why didn't you wave to me when I was on the train and waved to you. You were like a little marble Goddess. If you dont change we'll put you on a pedestal and keep you just to look at:

When I got home this morning I found Bopa still asleep; but he woke up and asked all about you and the "Girlies."

Now please write me a letter. All you have to do is to stand by Mother, or Bertha when her eyes are well and tell what you have been doing, or of a dream you've had, or what you think, and one of them will write it down for you.

Daddy

Father to Daughter

When Edward, Max and Charlie Perkins were, perhaps, eight, seven and six years old, they were very lively and totally beyond their mother's ability to control them. They were considered so wild that the neighbors in Windsor didn't want their boys to play with them. As a solution, their cousin Jerome Green was engaged for several summers to look after them. He was a college student. It was a great success. He roamed all over Windsor and Cornish with them, taught them to play tennis, baseball and kick the ball, told them stories and sang college songs. He made those summers so wonderful that our father relived them with his daughters years later.

He told us many stories about Cousin Jerome, who became a mythical hero to us. Bert and Peggy both remember the shock they felt when our father wrote in a letter that he had seen Jerome. It was as if he had said, "I ran into Achilles at the Harvard Club yesterday" — or Sir Lancelot, or D'Artagnan.

Tuesday July 22, [1919]

My Darling Bert: — Do write me some more nice long letters like the last one; and if you write any more of those little
stories, will you send them to me? I love to read them. When
I come again I will bring you the boat, and one for Peg and
one for Lisbeth. Tell me what you are reading now, and how
you like it.

That song Cousin Jerome sang was really sad, a little. I'll
show you the story it told in pictures. You see, both the Turk
and the Russian were so brave that each one killed the
other. It was a funny-sad song. Wait till you hear me sing it. I
have learned it by heart.

Bert, some of the ladies I saw when I was up at the house
had little girls; — but they were surprised when I told them
how my oldest little girl read such books as you read and
wrote me letters and read my letters. I was proud.

Daddy

Dear Peg: That was a nice letter you wrote me. I took it home to show to Bopa. Now send me another.

What do you do all the time — play with Jane when she is in her pen? Or play with the girlies or play with the frog like this?

I hope, when I come up again the red cheeks will have come. You must get them before you go back to Plainfield.

Daddy

Summers in Windsor

Tuesday, July 29, [1919]

Darling Bert: — Uncle Louis just telephoned to me. His ship came in this morning and he is just across the river in Camp Merritt. If he can he will come here to dinner and anyway he will come to see me tomorrow. Soon he will be in Windsor. He says he never sent Grandma a letter without addressing it himself. Will you tell her so?

I just tried to buy some boats but all the stores were closed for the night. But tomorrow I will try earlier and will send the boats by mail.

I tried to get Bopa to say he would go to Windsor next Sunday. He thinks Auntie Jean is lonely and that he ought to go to see her; but I know his four little grand-daughters are lonely for him.

Oh, I hope I'll get a letter from you tomorrow, my darling.

Daddy

Father to Daughter

Wednesday, August 7, [1919]

Darling Peg: — Cousin Lawrence says you got the boats and
that they sailed well. Do you think they did? Do you like

them? I ask you questions because then you will write to me.

It has been a rainy day here and very gloomy and all the
lights are lighted in this room though it is only afternoon;
and I am sitting now right under a lamp to write to you.

This club is a big house full of lonely daddies who want
to see their children and can't. They read newspapers and
play dominoes and think about their children.

Poor daddies! But if one of them gets a letter from one
of his children, why he is happy and proud. Daddy

Tuesday, September 2, [1919]

Darling Berta: — This must be a very short letter because I must go to see Bopa. I only wanted to tell you how proud I was of you when you wanted to go with us to the train and as soon as I whispered it would not be fair to E and Peg to take only you, you stopped asking right away. Then I was very proud of you, darling. I would rather have you just and fair than win prizes in school.

My! New York's a horrid place after Windsor. It's cloudy, and stuffy and smelly and noisy and rainy.

Your daddy

Darling Bert:
Yesterday I passed a shop window with models in it of just such ships as was the *Revenge*, and the ships that Raleigh and Amyas Leigh sailed in. I wish you had been with me.

I was on my way to see a remarkable man. Last fall when landlords were turning people out of their houses when they could not pay more rent, and there was no place where they could go, this man — a jew — held court and per-

suaded the landlords to let people stay. He was able to do it because he knew the way their hearts worked and didn't bother about their heads. That is, he didn't reason with

Father to Daughter

them. He knew their *reason* would say, "Get all the money you can when you have the chance." So he aimed at their hearts. His ways of doing this were wonderful and when he told them I was even a little attracted to him though he was so cheap and ugly, — more so than in the picture. Now this was one story.

A poor woman with five children came before him, and her landlady. The landlady had her little boy. She said: — "Judge, there ain't no use talkin. This woman's got five children and they are noisy and destructive. — They've got to go." (She was very cross and selfish looking.)

The Judge looked at the boy. "That's a *fine* boy you have," he said.

"He *is* a fine boy, Judge."

"You ought to be proud of that boy."

"I am Judge" said the lady straightening up and growing less cross.

Said the judge to the boy "Son you come up here. Get up on the bench. You be the judge" — and he put him in his chair.

"Now" he said to the boy "you know these children?"

"Yes" said the boy.

"You know" said the judge, "they'll have to go into the street. Theres no house for them anywhere, — but your mother has the right by law to put them out — "

Here the boy broke out — "I always thought Ma ought to leave 'em stay."

And the judge turned around quickly and said "It was written many centuries ago: 'and a little child shall lead them — '"

And the cross woman said "Here then gimme the lease. I'll keep 'em."

Wasn't that judge clever?

Your Daddy
P.S. Keep on with the poetry.

Saturday, September 6, [1919]

Darling Berta: I've just been for a walk with a lady, but she had on a skirt so tight she could hardly take a step. I had to keep waiting for her. I hope you wont wear such skirts when you are a lady. I told her you were a great walker and had climbed Mount Ascutney, 3000 feet high, and I thought no child so young had ever done it. She was a nice lady though:

　　　　　　　　　　　Father to Daughter

the skirt, she said, was the fault of the dress maker.

This is the way we went up Mt. Ascutney, — old Mother Ascutney, isn't it?

Daddy

Thursday, September 11, [1919]

Darling Lisbet: — You write me splendid letters. Please have another dream and tell me of it.

Have you been to the little log house since I left Windsor? If Miss Roberts or Mother took you there you could have lots of fun.

But what I want you to do is: Come home and take a walk with me.

Daddy

Sunday, September 14, [1919]

Darling E: — What a beautiful rainbow that must have been
I wish I had seen it too. This is you, looking at it.

E, a daddy can't have any fun without his children. There is no use his trying. Everywhere he goes he thinks, "Yes this would be fun if only my little girls were here; but what good is it without them." — He can't get them out of his head. He may go to see statues of something, but they are not what he really sees: — he sees his little girls, playing, far away. — But when he gets their letters, then he is happy.

Daddy

Father to Daughter

Monday, June 28, [1920]

Dear Zip: I went to the doctor's tonight by the street you take to go to school; and on the sidewalk by the bridge, in white crayon, was a picture like the one I have drawn.

Medor and I stopped and looked at it and said what we are saying in the picture, to ourselves. Did you? on the way to school.

Then I saw your school house, and the Markham children on the piazza, — a boy pushing himself around in an express cart, and two girls, one about your size and one smaller.

Yesterday in the woods we saw lots of children going on pic nics with their boxes and baskets and pails: — I wish they had been *you* children and going with me. When I saw the poor old lonely stone on the lawn yesterday, how I wished you were here to play "Kick-the-ball."

Daddy

Father to Daughter

Dear Bert: — I ain't much of a hand at writin, as Miss Watson says; but I will send you a letter if you want me to. You know I ain't had much schoolin. Every time I took a hold and started for school, why Tom would come along and say "Aw, Huck, come on and play hookey. I'm goin swimmin." And I would.

So I could not write this except Miss Watson was sitting by me knitting: She tells me how to spell all the words.

Well, Tom was telling me about this man Homer. He says he was a great poet but I think he was an awful liar, cause, for one thing, a hogs a hog and can't be nothing else, and we tested it. Tom got Mary to be a lady named Circe and gave her a stick which he said was a magic wand; and we went out where the hogs was. Tom said the hogs was his friends (he got awful mad when I laughed at that). He said he was Oddysseus and Circe had turned his friends, the

Summers in Windsor   61

brave Greeks, into hogs. And he told her to wave her wand and make them into men again; and she waved it, but it didn't do nothing to the hogs. I felt real sorry 'cause I almost thought they might change, specially when one grunted: Tom can make you believe anything. Tom was disappointed too; but Mary said, "Poor Tom! I guess you can't turn hogs into anything but ham, bacon, pork and sausages." But Tom said there were lots of other things we could do in the story of Oddysseus; — and then we went swimmin.

Your friend,
Huck Finn
Love to Peg and Liz

Father to Daughter

Wednesday

Dear Pegs: — This is a picture of you feeding the bottle lamb. Tomorrow I am going to buy canes for my three little girls. Tell Bert I think I can get ones to fit at the place where I got the boats, because that is a childrens store.

When I was out walking on Saturday in the woods I came upon camps like those of soldiers where people were living in tents out of doors. There were lots of children.

Then I came on a little log cabin without any glass in the windows and only one room, — about six children lived there.

Daddy

Our father was always interested in dreams and asked us about our dreams. In this too he was ahead of his time.

Saturday, August 15th

Darling E: — That was an interesting letter about your dream; — but I wish you would have nice dreams sometimes. Dont you ever?

At 4 o'clock today I looked at my watch and I said, — "even now I could catch that train to Windsor"; — and I almost went for it. But I knew it would be naughty for me to, and so I just barely didn't. Its as hard for daddys not be

naughty as it is for little girls. I will stay here and talk to Bopa but it will be very lonely. Maybe, next week we shall all be taking a walk together with our canes. But I cant be even sure of that.

Ask Uncle Louis if he wants to go up the mountain Saturday *above the hay fever line.*

Your Daddy

Father to Daughter

Tuesday, August 24

Darling Bert: —
I do not remember which
child I wrote to last so I will
begin over again with my
oldest. This is a picture of *us*
jumping off the float in our
bathing suits; — but I ought
to have made you holding
your nose.

Bopa and I went last night to the moving pictures. There
was one picture about a little boy. He was just going to play
ball when his mother called him to take a fine cake and a
letter to a sick man for his sister so he set out with the letter
in his cap and the cake in a card board box.

It was a hot day. He came to the house of a friend who
has stopped watering the lawn to soak his handkerchief in
water and put it in his cap so he would not get a sun stroke.
The little boy put his cake on the sidewalk and did this too.
He forgot the letter was in his cap; and the water from the
hose ran out on the sidewalk, all around the cake.

Then the boy went on till he met a lost dog. He decided to adopt the dog, so he had to carry the cake under one arm and the dog under the other.

Father to Daughter

This was hard so he sat down once to rest; and the dog
got interested in the box which was soft from the water.

So when he got to the sick man and the man opened the

cake and the letter, he wrote to the boys sister: — "Thanks
very much. But please tell me what it was you sent me and
what you said in your letter."

Wasn't that a funny picture.

Daddy

In the following letter, our father has dressed himself up like Pretty Boy to tease Zippy.

Wednesday, August 25, [1920]

Darling E: —
Have you forgiven me for teasing you so much? You know its because I love you that I do it; so please write me and say you

are not angry. I wish, when I wake up in the morning now there was a "*you*" to come in and talk to me, the way you did in Windsor.

Father to Daughter

But I have to get up all alone — don't even see Bopa —
and go to breakfast all alone: there is no one to talk to but
the waiter in a waiters suit.

So, please get Bertha to sit down at the desk and write
you a letter for me.

Daddy

This letter tells about one of the first times Max Perkins suggested a plot to a writer—it became one of his strengths. Many writers have said that he was responsible for starting them on a new book.

Tuesday, August 31, [1920]

Darling Bert: — Your letter came today. I know, darling, when you write letters for the others you can't write so many yourself. I was ever so glad to hear from you though.

This picture shows me doing what I have been doing for five whole hours — talking. I have been trying to tell a writer and his wife how he should write. Isn't that funny when I don't know how to do it myself. I even told him a story *to* write that I made up; — and he was delighted with it. Its pretty hard to talk all the evening about things you don't know anything about. But I told them about you too. The thing on the chin of the lady is a bandage: she was in a taxi-cab collision today and was badly cut.

Father to Daughter

Here are the beggar girl and boy asleep on the King's grounds and the beautiful Queen and the fat little prince are just finding them. The gardeners are looking at them. I hope you will think of another story to tell me.

Daddy

Uncle Louis and I had a swim in the pool and then we had a dinner. Uncle Edward has a baby boy, one day old. I suppose you heard this before. We'd rather have boys for *cousins* than for brothers wouldn't we? These are good enough boys for us, aren't they

Daddy

Wednesday,
September 1st [1920]

Darling E: —
Is this the way you looked
when you dressed up like a
farmer? I guess you did look
funny. I wish I had seen you.
Did the others dress up that
way too?

You wouldn't think it was
hard but the thing that
makes me tiredest is talking
and I have been doing nothing else this week; — so I am
tired.

Then last night I had quite an attack of hay fever: I had
to get up and walk up and down Bopa's study. So, I can't
write you much of a letter tonight.

Your Daddy

Darling Bert: — The story about the Black Douglas was ever so good. I love to have you write these stories. I wonder if I shall get another before I come up on Friday.

When I was visiting on Sunday, we all went swimming in a pond. And there was a platform you could dive from. And a little girl with freckles like E, but more and bigger went in. She was just nine; but she could swim and didn't mind going under water, head and all. She would stand on the platform, give a jump and splash into quite deep water.

One of the mothers there said she had a daughter, fifteen, who loved horses. But they couldn't afford to give her one. They noticed that she was saving all the money they gave and was earning money one way and another. One day she went out and when she came back she was leading a horse. She had bought it. And from that day she has fed, watered and cleaned that horse herself.

Your Daddy

Black Douglas

Darling Bert: —

This is Daddy eating dinner at a Chinese restaurant — rice and chop suey and tea — with a waiter in black pajamas and a pig tail. They will give you chop sticks if you want them.

The man who wrote *The Hidden People* has now written a story about a panther. I suggested that he try animal stories and he is going to send me this one. I wish you and I could read it together. I didn't have any letter from you so I read over the *Guy of Gisborne* story again.

Your Daddy

Darling Peg, I'm going to send you the first letter, because you're the youngest, except Jane. The House is still here, and Medor, and William's dog are barking; but they wont wake any children in this house.

Medor and I walked over to the Doctors, and he panted so hard from the heat that he shook all over, all the way.

Then he innoculated me, while Medor waited outside: I could hear him panting.

Please write me: tell me how it was to sleep in a train and how you like the little farm house.

Daddy

Tuesday

Darling Peg: —

One day when I was a little boy I thought I would play Indian. I got an axe handle for a club, and a bow and arrow, and turkey feathers to make a headdress with, and then paints to paint my face. And I made green and red streaks all over my face; — and I had the hair of a doll for my scalp It was lots of fun — that day.

But the next day my face was all speckled as if with measles, and it itched and itched; and my eyelids swelled up so I couldn't see. — The paint had poisoned me. I had to stay in bed for several days with wet cloths on my face — there was no fun in *that* and I never painted up like an Indian again. Don't you ever do it either.

Daddy

When he went back to New York, our father would leave each one of us with a poem to learn and recite to him when he came back.

Father to Daughter

Friday, June 24th [1921]

Darling Berta: —

I've just walked to and from the doctor's with Medor who seems to amuse everyone. Why is that? Because he is fat? You might think he was a moon dog. He sits on the doctor's piazza while I am inside, and I leave my cane with him as a pledge that I will surely come back.

This is the way I think of you now, learning poetry; — and I got your letter darling, Zipper's too, and was ever so happy. But now you have be-gun on the *Ancient Mariner* you must finish it and its very long. I learned it all once in school and had to recite from it in an oral examination. Have you enough books to read?

When you write again, tell me what the place is like and what all of you do.

Bert, its so hot that I think I'll sleep on the piazza tonight.
Daddy

Tuesday, August 30th,
1921

Darling Zipper: —
I'm going to the movies tonight to see the best story in
the world — *The Three Musketeers.* This is the way the men
in it dressed, — with feathers in their hats, and long
curls. If they weren't in a
fight they were looking for
one.

This is the way they fought, — with long thin swords
called rapiers. I'll read you the story some time.

I know just what you are doing now. You and Peg are
climbing into your chairs at the supper table. Miss Roberts
is telling Bertha to put down her book and come too. Jane is
trying to catch the Kitty under the table instead of taking
her seat, and Nellie is putting the dishes before you. This is
Shreaded Wheat and as soon as you taste it you will say —
delicious!

Your Daddy

Zippy wanted to be a princess. When we made our wish lists at Christmas she always wished for a golden crown, and Bert for a suit of armor. Mother would produce the golden crown, made from cardboard and painted bright gold. The suit of armor never came.

Zippy was very intense and inclined to fall deeply in love with young men who were dressed up and showing off to their flapper girlfriends. Our father used to tease her by calling them "Pretty Boys" and saying that anything they could do he could do better.

Zippy was also thrown into despair because she had a light dusting of freckles on her nose. They were charming, but nobody else had them. He laughed gently at her for this, too.

Thursday, July 7, [1922]

Darling Zipper: —
This is daddy vaulting the post, so easy and graceful, as if it were nothing at all. And it isn't, for me. Now look at Mr. Pretty-Boy trying what he can do, on the other side of the paper.

See that! Never got over at all. Now what do you think of your Pretty-Boy? When I was sixteen, I used to jump over that white farm house at the foot of Washington Rock Hill, and think nothing of it at all. Ask Uncle Louis. Here's a picture to prove it.

I had to stop while a man told me what a fine daughter he had. Zipper, she's not half as good as you, I'll bet. You might think she was Helen of Troy to hear him talk. What does he know of girls with only one?

Why I have a daughter
You'd think a Princess
When dressed in her prettiest clothes.
Though I must with reluctance
And sorrow confess
She has freckles all over her nose.

Zipper, you know I love your freckles, and everybody does; and Princesses always have them because they show a delicate skin. In fact, I don't think they would allow a girl *without* freckles to *be* a princess, for a princess must be *excessively* delicate. So now write me a letter for saying such nice things about you. If you don't *soon* I'll send you one showing Mr. Pretty-Boy being bucked by a bull.   Your Daddy

Monday, July 10th

Darling Peg,

I had to run for my train last night, down the hill to the station. But my berth was all ready for me and in ten minutes I was in bed and asleep; and when I woke I was almost in New York. Its a horrid place, after Windsor, Peg — if I were in the best place in the world and you were in the worst I'd write you *lots* of letters.

Then I went to be innoculated against hay fever. Heres a picture of it happening. But there was one thing that made

me happy — the letters from my chicadees, the long one from you. That was worth coming back for.

This is *us* going to Pasture Hill — you are in front the way you really were.

Daddy

Tuesday, July — 1922

Zipper darling:
It's raining again: rained yesterday too. How is it with you.
This is you racing at the pic-nic, and winning the race too.

I called on a lady today
and she told me about her
nieces, 9 and 12. They were
upstairs alone undressing.
The oldest looked into her
fathers room and saw this —
a burglar! She said nothing
to her sister for she knew the
sister would scream. But she
went quietly down the back
stairs and told her daddy.
Wasn't she brave. He got a
pistol and went up, but the
burglar heard him and
climbed out a window. I said
I thought Bert would do just
that same thing. Don't you
think so?

Father to Daughter

This is *you* playing Badminton and Jane looking on.
Now I must play checkers with Uncle Louis.

Your Daddy

Wednesday, July 26th, 1922

Darling Pegs: — Are you well now? Do you go swimming?
Now Zip has learned it's your turn you know, — and then
Janey's.

I sent for my bathing suit because I must spend Saturday
and Sunday with a man and his wife on the seashore. His
name is Gregory and he has two boys, and he dedicated his
last book to me. — Peg, I don't want to go there but I *must,*
sometime. Perhaps its best to do it and be done with it.

This is Bert jumping off the float.

Oh, Peg, suppose I looked up, in this big, darkish room,
full of deadly men with their hats on, and saw you coming
over too me with that Mona Lisa smile of yours. Wouldn't I
be happy though, all of a sudden. I'd give you lots of fun
Peg, — a fine cake and ice cream dinner; and then to the the-
ater. And I'd put you on the train to Windsor in the morning
and Mother would meet you at 3 P.M. Why not do it?

Daddy

Father to Daughter

The Palace of Gloom
August 8th, 1922

Peggoty darling, My days are like so many sheep going over a fence, — so there's not much to write letters about.

Here I am getting a hair cut and hearing about the hair crops and how much greater they become in September.

Here I am looking for my suit and not finding it; — and then later I telephoned Uncle Louis and he had it on because it was better pressed than any he had and he would have brought it home if he had come himself: — Yes, if he didn't come home in his underclothes. Now I can tell whether its a nice suit or not, by seeing someone else in it.

Here I am listening to Mrs. Tutweiler talk about Mothers plays: — she wants other copies. Has Mother got any of any of them? And did Mr. Swartout have them copyrighted?

But, Pegs, I got no letters today — and you told me you would write me one. Please do it.

Your Daddy

August 16th, 1922

Darling Berta: — I'm so sorry you were sick and missed *The Three Musketeers*, — but you'll like the book better for it when you read it.

D'Artagnan was a brave, earnest, ambitious young man, — not a playful school boy as they make him in the play. And Athos, — he was a real man, greater than D'Artagnan: in the play he is a stuffed bolster.

He was much older than D'Artagnan and advised and helped him. He was wise, and just and noble, not a hot head. I'll read the book to you in the winter if you'll let me. — And the Cardinal too is rather a fine man in the book; — he was a *great man* you know, really. He made France into a nation; — it had been a collection of little Dukedoms and Earldoms.

D.Artagnan.   Athos

Bert, its so hot! Do you know what I'm going to do? Go to the apartment, get into pajamas and read there, — like this.

Dearest one, I want to see you ever so much.

Daddy

Father to Daughter

August 17th, 22

Darling Zip:
I just bought my ticket to Windsor for tomorrow night. Will
it ever come?

Yes I did get that letter, and it was beautiful, and you are
my angel child. Beatrice Rhoades who went on that pic nic
Sunday asked about you and Berta. She's a flipperty,
flopperty flapper Zip. Don't you ever be one. They're *so*
silly. Beatrice seemed to think you were a *mischevious* girl.
How could she. You, my angel child.

Here's one of those musketeers Zip. Aren't they great fellows. I used to love them. Athos was the best of the lot, — or else Cyrano de Bergerac. Poor Cyrano. He used to say he liked to have enemies, — they helped him to walk straight.

He loved a girl; but he was so ugly on account of his enormous nose, he knew she would never look at him, but rather at one of your pretty boys. But this Mr. Pretty Boy couldn't make love so Cyrano did it for him — to the girl *he* loved and won her for Monsieur Pretty Boy. Wasn't that sad?

Your Daddy

Father to Daughter

This letter and the next were written from Bar Harbor, Maine. Our father was visiting Arthur Train, a well-known writer. It was probably a working visit.

September 16th, 1924

Darling Berta: — This is a splendid rugged country, sombre with black pines; with hemlocks and cedars. The islands that rise out of the blue sea are great roundbacked rocks whose tops bristle with evergreens. There are seven or eight mountains on the island which also are rocks, huge ridges of rock: when you get to the top you can walk along them there for two miles or so, above the sea. I have climbed four including the highest, one this morning. — And one we climbed on the mainland, the best of all. You stood on the edge of a precipice and looked over a blackish green ocean of tree tops, quite unbroken by cultivation in some directions; — in others you could make out a green meadow here and there; but really it was exactly as it was to the first white man. Here and there the soft sea of pine tops was indented by the hard surface of a lake. — But Bert, I've either got hay-fever badly, or a cold. I can't decide which, but last night was very bad. If Mother had been here I would have kept her awake. But if it's hay fever, it can't last much longer and if its a cold, it ought to be well in a day or two. Only the remembrance of your patient endurance got me through the night; I was for jumping out of bed every minute.

I've been kept very busy, — have had no time to write, except one note to Mother; and if anyone is going to write me they had better do it quick for I expect to leave in six days more.

Your loving Daddy

Bar Harbor
[Visiting Arthur Train] Sunday, October 17, 1925

Darling Pegs: —

Yesterday morning it poured. In the afternoon it stopped but fog hid the mountains. The whole party went for a walk but I branched off and climbed a Mt. alone. It was warm and still at first but when I got to the vast bare rock that forms the summit a gale that I had to brace against was sweeping the tattered fog across and it was bitter cold. Sometimes the gale would drive me several feet. It was exciting. Once in a while the fog would be driven off below and I looked down upon a saffron forest, — all-in-yellow. When I got down it was almost dark and I was lost. But I found a high road and a man took me into his motor and brought me to a place I knew.

Today we went in motors away inland to climb a big hill. I and a lady came down ahead, and I got lost again. I hallooed and far away we heard an answer. — So we got our direction and went that way, and called again, and gradually got nearer, and at last came to a field where the pic nic was waiting.

Mother has a fine time breakfasting in bed every day. — But she doesn't care much for the mountains.

Now I must hurry and dress for dinner.

How I wish I was with you all in New Canaan.

Father to Daughter

On one of our weekend walks, Peggy fell and broke her collarbone. Our father was always very upset when anybody was suffering, and he was concerned about this until he knew she was well again. He sent her a book by Hector Malot called Nobody's Girl, *in appreciation of her courage.*

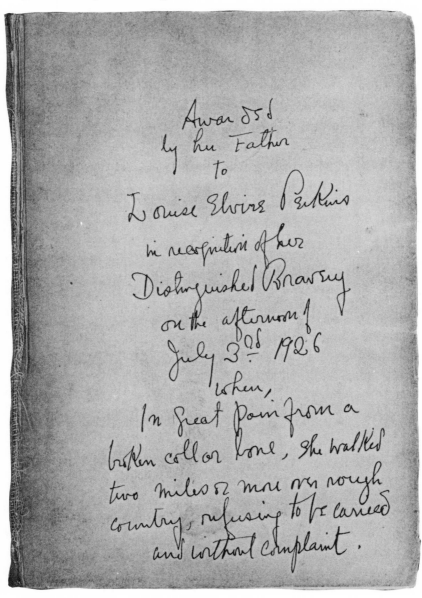

Awarded
by her Father
to

Louise Elvira Perkins

in recognition of her

Distinguished Bravery

on the afternoon of

July 3rd 1926

when,

In great pain from a
broken collar bone, she walked
two miles or more over rough
country, refusing to be carried
and without complaint.

July 13th, 1926

Darling Zippy: —
Here is a picture of poor
Peg, with her arm bound up.
— But I ought not to draw
for you anymore. You are
learning really to draw and
ought not to look at bad pictures. Did mother tell you?
— I asked Mr. Parrish about
copying. He said it was a
good thing to do, a little.
Did you draw the big man
and the fat, round lady?

These elevateds Zippy, — they grate, and roar, first on
one side, then the other.

Father to Daughter

The boys play baseball on this street. They've marked out a long, narrow diamond with chalk. Nobody has such fun as boys have when a motor comes, they just barely slip out of the way, and jump back to their places the next minute; — and I guess they have to keep an eye open for "cops." The great thing about a boy is he is an outlaw without disgrace. A man feels ashamed, and of course that spoils all the fun.

This is Daddy writing to you, in pajamas, by the open window. I hope some time you will write to me; but you are the busiest girl of all this summer with Arithmetic, drawing and the Banjo-uke.

Your Daddy

Summers in Windsor   93

Billy Buttfield, Mother's nephew, was the nearest thing we had to a brother. A diary entry of Peggy's from July 16, 1929 reads, "Today we went out with Bill to catch turtles and how many do you think we caught? 35!! He taught us how to handle the net. He is so reckless. He plunges his whole arm in! Once he put his whole head in! This afternoon we swam." Bill was first pilot of a B-29 bomber. He was killed over Japan in 1945.

July 19th, 1926

Berta Darling:

I've just left the office and I've come here because I'm almost sure to see nobody I know; — in fact there's only one person in this big, gloomy room, and he too old, sleepy, and whiskery to recognize his own brother; so I can quietly write you a letter before I myself go to sleep.

Billy and I got berths as soon as we reached Claremont Junction (my electric light just burned out and I had to change it.) We got a lower and upper and Billy had already announced he wanted to sleep in a lower. I could have dissuaded him by saying that his cousins all thought more highly of an upper (which is a kind of pun I'll point out) but I thought better of it for two reasons: (1.) I never saw Bill still for an instant; when I visualized him asleep it was, *wriggling;* and I thought he was pretty certain to fall out, and if from an upper, there would be another broken collar bone; and (2.) the way those turtles were acting, I thought they were likely soon to be at large, and if in an upper, they might well slip through into the lower where a lady would perhaps be, "— and Then Oh! and Then Oh!" — as the man sang in song about the frog and the duck that we used to hear in Whooping Cough days.

So then we ate our supper and I took the box with the egg shells etc. to the rear platform and threw it out and looked back. The sun was shining again, and it was fresh and cool and damp and misty. And there was old Ascutney all silvery in mist; and I thought: "What a fool not to wait till the midnight."

When Bill consented to go to bed I showed him about the light in his berth, and what to do with his clothes and all, and I said: "When you feel someone poking you and pulling at your blanket, it will be the porter telling you to get up. Then say 'alright' and go to sleep." In the morning I looked in on him and found him dressed and he said, "I tried to do what you said, Uncle Max, but he came back and poked me again."

We had breakfast at Bopa's. When I had to go I could find Bill nowhere in the house, and so I tried the garden. He was by the big fountain in the middle of it exercising his turtles. It was cool in the garden, and the sunlight shone through the willow tree upon the fountain, so that the bottom of the bowl was dappled with light and shade. I guess the turtles felt that they had got to a real place after a night in a glass jar.

We talked about various mss. this afternoon, and there was one about bridges. It had almost every bridge you could think of from that notorious one Caesar built across the Rhine to the Queensboro bridge; — but not the Windsor Bridge, and so I knew it was a poor book, and declined it.

I'm so glad you're reading *Henry Esmond* again. If you have time to write me do it, darling.

Your Daddy

P.S. Tell Miss Lemmon I *did* mail her letters. I know she thinks I didn't, by telepathy. *M.E.P.*

Magic Lanterns *was a collection of one-act plays by Louise Saunders, our mother. She wrote many plays, short stories and poems which were published in* Scribner's *and other magazines.*

Both our parents loved children and were interested in all of us, but they were very different. With Mother, life was exciting, wonderful, magical. She did unexpected and amazing things for us. Once, on a rather boring ordinary day, she came in clapping her hands, and cried, "Oh children! Come! Come out to the sandbox. I have something to show you!" We demurred. What could be interesting about the sandbox? But we went. It looked as usual except for four brand new little pails and shovels. She gave one to each of us and told us to dig. Bewildered, we dug and began to discover exquisite little toys buried in the sand! We dug faster and faster, until our pails were full of magical presents. We never quite knew how they got there.

She loved to play practical jokes. One April Fool's Day we had our supper as usual at a little table in the dining room, while our governess, Miss Roberts, read to us. We dutifully ate Wheatina or oatmeal and finished it only because dessert was coming. But when it came, this time, it was only a poached egg on toast. This was not to be borne! We had done our part. All of us objected noisily. "That's not fair. We ate our cereal!" On examination, dessert turned out to be a piece of pound cake with an apricot on top, surrounded by whipped cream. It was very good, and we were embarrassed.

On a hot summer morning, Mother would say, "Oh, children! Look! The fairies had a picnic on the lawn last night." And there were their tablecloths: tiny gossamer cloths of silvery dew.

It was Miss Roberts who took care of all the humdrum routine of daily life and gave us total security.

July 28, 1926

Peggoty darling

Is all right with you and the collar bone? Maybe I'll hear
from some of you tomorrow. I'll hurry to the office to see if
any of the Girlies have written me. In this picture I am buy-
ing a ticket for Friday on the train that gets in about mid-
night. Tell Mother so she can tell Grandma not to lock me
out. Here I am talking to the man who is to do pictures for
Mother's story. Tell Mother his name is *Shenton*, — she
knows him; — and I chose him because I like his pictures.
He'll do these on a ship on the way to Mexico.

I wrote Cousin Helen a long letter last night. She is ill you know. I told how we swam in the Queechy. She loves Windsor so. Why don't you and Zip write her. It would make her happy to know you were playing in Windsor just as she and we cousins played there. She was the best of the lot at Knock the Stick, and now what! — lie still and have her temperature taken. Write her Peg! We should all have done it long ago.

This is meant to be Billy. Bopa saw him on Saturday when he came in to go to the Pratts. They are on Long Island. I guess it was too slow for him in Plainfield. He was glad to go there anyway.

Tell Mother I ordered that six copies of *Magic Lanterns* should be sent her. I did it on the very morning I arrived from Windsor. — So dont be angry with *me* if they haven't come. Be angry with President Coolidge.

Your Daddy

Helen's address is Trudeau Sanitarium, Trudeau, New York

Father to Daughter

Copeland's Treasury for Booklovers *was an anthology of English and American poetry and prose writing put together by Charles T. Copeland, Boylston Professor of Oratory and Rhetoric at Harvard College. "Copey," as he was called, was the professor who inspired our father and aroused his interest in literature.*

July 29th, 1926

Berta darling: — I got your letter and the line I first saw was that which said "He says Peggy's bone is together now"; and that was what I wanted most to hear. Once the plaster is off she can go swimming with a sling just for that.

This is a drip, drip, drippy day. Not exactly rain, but worse. A man can't decide whether an umbrella or the drizzle is the worse; and so gets wet, the drizzle coming easier. The sidewalks and the streets shine, and the motors swish through the scum. And everything is damp and sticky. Is it so in Windsor?

Summers in Windsor

Bert, what a wonderful man Hamlet was. I was reading some proof in Copey's reader. What things he said! What equal has he in all literature and history? Could Shakespeare talk as he did, — think and feel as he did? If Jack Barrymore ever plays him again, or anyone else that plays him well, you and I shall see it.

I just went for a hair-cut, in spite of Bopa. He says any man can cut his own hair, — with clippers. And I almost believe him, but not quite; and one reason I don't is that (between you and me) his own hair looks a bit ragged. But I do think a barber could cut our hair in two minutes, if he would, with clippers. Mine could give no real argument against it. He temporized, — and didn't do it.

I think these clubs are dreadful places, full of black shadows of gloom. The men mostly play dull games like dominoes day after day after day. There's Arnold Frazer-Campbell, tall and handsome and brave; and he was in the Black Watch, in kilts, and lost an arm, and got decorated; and he has sunk to this life in death of dominoes day after day. He is from Windsor too, or Cornish. He has seen Windsor and he has seen war and can dribble his life away in dominoes in a gloomy club. — And the Century is worse for there they all go to sleep behind their newspapers and their beards. I marvel that in former years I could spend two weeks solid in New York in the summer. — But, when I came here to be a reporter it seemed a veritable City of Bagdad and I could not have too much of it.

Well, I'll pack my bag tonight, and take it to the office tomorrow; and I'll leave for Windsor on the 5:02 train which is due to arrive at 11:50. But, Bert, that swimming in the Queechy with so many children is too dangerous. We mustn't do it.

Your loving Daddy

After Bopa retired, he lived at 246 East 49th Street, and our father stayed there while we were in Windsor. He had a monkey named Jocko on a long chain in the conservatory, and a blue parrot who talked constantly.

Mother often directed the cousins in one-act plays she had written. One of them was The Knave of Hearts, *which Maxfield Parrish saw and suggested to Scribners that he illustrate.*

August 3rd, 1926

Darling Pegs: —
Is this the way you are now, with your arm in your sleeve? I can't remember. — But it must be so, or how could you wear a sling? And soon there will not even be a sling, and Peggy will be as free as any, and able to go anywhere and do anything again.

This is meant to be Jocko, but it's not a good portrait. I never drew a monkey before. I'll have to look at him carefully and consider him. No one can draw or write without that. The hand is nothing, the eye is *all.* I guess that's the way with acting too: if you get a thing *right* in your brain, you will get it right on paper, or on the stage. — Excuse me for preaching.

This is a picture of the way I felt when I noticed I was preaching. Thats the way Fathers used to do in the olden days. — But then there were fewer men in the world so that they thought they were of more importance than we can now'a days.

How is the play going. You children must try to help Mother so that she wont get too tired. Its so hot and she hates the heat so. Here it's 94°.

A great lady swimmer came in today. — She's writing a book for us about swimming — and I told her the best swimming in the world was in the Queechy River. She was surprised. She had never heard about it. — I told how the girlies swam through the rapids.

Your loving Daddy

Father to Daughter

August 4, 1926

Darling Janey:

Here am I writing to you in the heat; and wishing I were with you in the pond. And you six years old now and a school girl! I know what your presents were like for Zippy drew pictures of them all. I sent you a book, and now I'm afraid you had it already. — *The Adventures of Nils*. But then I can bring it back and get you another. I know you are to have a water horse for this is what she said to me when I left her in New York on Monday.

I have my ticket for Windsor on the same train I came up on last week. Where am I to sleep? In Mother's house or Grandma's house. I guess in Mother's, and I'll go there first and see if there is a note to tell me, and if not, that will be right. Bopa and Jocko and the Parrot all go by motor to Cape May on Friday. — Thats the place Bert and Zippy and Peg went to right after you were born: Miss Roberts took them and they played on the beach. — This is the way they all looked.

Your Daddy

August 17, 1926

Darling Pegs: — Here are you and Molly about to go swimming in the brook, — which you must never, never again do. And so you've promised. I got a letter from Bert today which said it was *cold* in Windsor. I hope it still is. Here it is hot, and steaming with the damp. Every day it rains.

This colored cook! She thinks men ought to eat enormous meals. When I thought I had finished breakfast today, in she came with a plate of waffles; and as I was finishing that, in she came with another. Here I am sneaking out with the last two in my handkerchief. I couldn't eat them. — Nor could I eat any lunch!

Father to Daughter

I went today to the Hispanic Museum and saw some wonderful Spanish pictures of bulls and bullfighters and knights and ladies and I thought, how Pegs would love it. I'll take you there someday, and then to the Indian Museum which is next door.

I have bought my ticket, Pegs, for Windsor, for Friday night.

Your Daddy

August 31, 1926

Darling Pegs: —

I must take a walk. I'm to dine with an author, and he has ordered the dinner at the Coffee House; and how am I to eat it? — for I had lunch with another author and he ate so much that I had to eat more than I wanted to be polite. How can any one eat in New York anyway?

I thought I had Hay Fever, but now its so much better that I guess it was a cold. I hope so. I was up and tramping the floor quite a bit last

night. Oh, I'll be glad if it is only a cold! I'd begun to think of moving to the top of Mt. Ascutney. Don't you like my pajamas? I thought I might as well make 'em pretty in the picture, whatever they really are.

Peg's, there's a book in my room by Swift. Can't you take it carefully up to the White House yourself and give it to Aunt Mary? Here you go.

Your Daddy

Hay Fever Chorus
Tramp, Tramp, Tramp,
the boys are marching:—
The dear old rag weed is in bloom:
And we'll sneeze and sneeze and sneeze
In the Cool September breeze
As we tramp and tramp and tramp across the room—
A-Ker-Choo!

Father to Daughter

PEG'S VISIT

*In 1926, Peggy stayed behind in Windsor and visited our grand-
mother for two months. As always, our father wrote to her regularly.*

September 12th, 1926

Darling Peg: How can you treat us so, — and we wondering
about you so often. Please do write to us. Tell us: did you get
a green dress, a red dress, and a dark blue skirt with a green
and yellow sweater? Mother sent them and she must find out.

Last night as we were all sitting around the fire there
came a great, sudden commotion on the piazza — growls,
thumps, meows. I rushed out. Nothing there! But below the
sound of creatures rushing round and then, when I
shouted, the shapes of two dogs slinking off. Zip got a
candle. We went down to look for Kissy. We called. We held
the candle up and looked into the trees. We could see and
hear nothing. So we gave up.

But when Zip woke in the morning she heard me-owing. High up in a tree was puss. With the help of a step ladder she climbed the tree. She took a paper bag and stuffed puss in and climbed down. Near the bottom, the bag burst and out fell Kissy. But she was well, and glad to get down, and Zip comforted her.

Tonight, Zip had long gone to bed. It was cold. I was by the fire. I heard a slight noise and looked toward the door. There was Zippy in her nightgown. She'd remembered the bird was out on the piazza. It was lucky she did on so cold a night.

Oh, Peg, please do write us.

Your Daddy

September 18th, 1926

Darling Pegs: — You see, Mother told the Windsor post office, when we left, to forward all mail to New Canaan. So they began to forward, or really *backward* my letters to you. They returned to us. And then Mother wrote on them "do not send back to New Canaan" and mailed them again.

Mother has gone to a dance at the Perry's; — a farewell dance, for they are to leave New Canaan. They must live in Chicago now. As for me, I shall go to bed when I finish this letter.

Here are Zippy and Janey on the rocks at the Rhoades, fishing this afternoon. Each of them caught one fish but too small a one to keep.

Bert, sat on the rocks too, but she read; — and Mother and I had tea on the piazza with Mr. Rhoades and looked out over the wide shining sound.

This is your friend, Franklin McWilliams. I saw him a day or two ago. Do you remember, his brother had hay fever so terribly? But he did not have it this year his father told me because he was innoculated. Isn't that good?

Your loving Daddy

Father to Daughter

September 23rd, 1926

Darling Pegs: — This is Mother sewing by the fire, now. She has taken to brushing her hair straight back, which is much better. I have just finished reading *War and Peace* to Zip. — Next year I'll read it to you.

Berts school began today and she was late. — But it wasn't her fault, for she was ready to start in time. She is to read Caesar, in latin, and I shall help her, which will be fun. Caesar looked something like this. He was bald headed. He was one of the greatest men and greatest soldiers that ever lived, and this book Bert is to read is his own story of his wars. He didn't do very much till he was over forty, except dance and be generally silly, — play games that correspond to bridge and golf and frequent places like our country clubs. Then, I always

thought, he got so disgusted with these things and the people who do them, that he went out into the wilderness and led the Roman armies in many battles. He wanted to do something healthy and hard, whatever it was.

Here is Jules, Mary's husband. He waits on the table now and she cooks. Emma went away because she was lonely without any colored people to talk to.

Your loving Daddy

September 26th, 1926

Darling Pegs: — I enclose the verses Jane and Zippy sang, and Zippy wrote, on my birthday. I know yours is coming soon. We all do. — Before I forget it: Bert says she left a Frazier and Square French Grammer in mothers room in Windsor. Can you find it and send it to her.

It is cold today; but yesterday how hot it was, — like July; and here we are, swimming off the Rhoades rocks. The tide

Father to Daughter

was high and the water cool and a wind was blowing. Jane paddled around in her waterwings and floated on the old cork fish and Bert dived from a high ledge. She wore Mother's suit.

The Ellsworth and the Kellogg girls were there and Bert rowed them in the flat bottom boat over the waves. It was great fun. — And then at night came a roaring, crashing thunder storm and the lights went on and off, and the lightning flashed and flickered, and it grew cold. No more swimming! Skating next.

Jen and I went for a walk and Jen wore her new winter coat. But it wasn't cold enough for that by the time we'd climbed the long stoney hill by the rock where we have pic nics. So we hid the coat behind a stone wall. We walked around the lake where the white rock is, and were going home another way when, just in time, Jane remembered the coat. She was afraid we had lost it, but it was there as good as ever.

Your loving Daddy

Mary Colum was a critic; her husband, Padraic, a writer and poet.
They lived in New Canaan for a while and often came to the house.

October 7th, 1926

Darling Pegs: — I haven't written you for several days. Tuesday night we went to the Righter's for Mr. Righter's birthday, where there was champagne and a cake with candles, and we didn't get home till almost one; and last night came Mr. and Mrs. Atterbury from Plainfield who left at ten; and then Mr. Colum, with a silver pin for you and one for Janey, just home from Ireland, with Wang. They stayed till eleven, and Wang went all over the house, even I suppose into the room of Zip and Janey though they didn't know it. He's a wild dog. Mrs. Colum was coming out of her door and Wang rushed at it and banged it shut on her foot, and it broke her toe, her *little* toe. — But they like him. — I suppose Mother will send you the pin, and you must then thank Mr. Colum.

Now Mother has gone to the movies with the Righters and I have just finished reading to Zip from *War and Peace.* It was about a battle and I laid out matches to show how the Russian and French troops were arranged. Here we are.

Father to Daughter

Bert too was listening. You must hear it too, for in it is the best man that ever was written about except perhaps Hamlet. He is Prince Andrei. I wish each of you, if you *must* marry, would find a Prince Andrei for a husband. — Even if he is a little too scornful and impatient.

Did you suggest to Miss Ulen that you might write a long letter for a composition? I wish you could for your letters are good and interesting, but they're short. Do you play with the Thomases every day? And how is Spotty? I've bought you a birthday present and I think you will like it.

Your loving Daddy

This is you writing me a letter.

October 9th, 1926

Darling Pegs: —

David Hall was in the apple tree behind the school. He meant to drop from a limb to the ground but lost his grip and fell too soon. He landed on his back with his arm under him. It was broken in several places and the first doctor they took him too set it badly and Dr. O'Shaunnessy had to do it all over again.

Here we are going to the Yale-Princeton Game on next Saturday. Bopa sent the children tickets. Next year I must take you to a game.

Its raining. There never was a rainier day. And there have been many. — Yet, the reservoirs are so low that in my walks I keep to the woods and so avoid them: — they look sick and boney with strange rocks sticking up gaunt heads near the shore and four or five feet of sand and stones bared around the rims. I took Zip and Janey on a long, long walk on Saturday. It was a summer day. Jane liked two parts of it especially: a sloping field of long yellow grass with many slim birch trees along the edges, which looked like Russia; and a high, hilly plateau where there were big rocks, half buried, which looked like Scotland. It was dark before we got back to the car, and two stars were out, far apart, — a golden one and a red one. Jane saw the red one first and Zippy, the yellow one.

This is me talking to a man who has written a book called *Singing Soldiers*. I think he has a wooden leg. When he was in the war he collected all the songs he could hear, mostly those of negroes. I think it is going to be a really good book.

Your loving Daddy

P.S. I saw Mr. Hall on the train and he told me the truth about David: — This apple tree has branches around it at fairly equal intervals. The boys try to swing from one to another like squirrels; they call it the squirrel act. David was the best squirrel of all; — but this time he missed his hold and fell.

He had to do as you did with the collar bone, go to the hospital and have ether and X-rays; — but he didn't mind ether and wasn't sick from it. And now all will be right with him if he can keep quiet.

Daddy

October 11th, 1926

Darling Pegs: — *I* thought your writing was much better as soon as I saw the letter to Zip. I meant to tell you so. It is much better than only a couple of weeks ago.

Yesterday was a foggy, drippy day, — rain, mist, rain. We could do nothing but read. Jane came down wrapped in blankets and sat on the sofa before the fire. And then the Hamilton's called and she tried to escape, and barely did with the blankets trailing after her. She is much better and may go out tomorrow, — if it is sunny, which today it was. I sent your present today and Bopa sent one too, — a super-fine one. I guess you'll have a good birthday.

Here is Janey listening to the end of the story of the mouse colored gelding. We have just three pages left for to-morrow night. The next book will be *The Children of New Forest*. — We are making a holiday edition of that for the Christmas after this one. I wish you could first have read it with those fine pictures.

Well, this is the next thing, Pegs. Off to Bar Harbour. — And I swear I shall never, never do it again.

Your loving Daddy

Father to Daughter

That year our mother and father went to visit the Arthur Trains at Bar Harbor, Maine.

October 20th, 1926

Darling Pegs: — Here we are. Its very cold and clear. Mother's still in bed, where she has her breakfast. Later we shall go out and climb a Mountain. On Sunday we walked. We came to a field and saw something move. It was a fox, caught in a trap by the toes of his hind leg. We opened the trap and he galloped off across the fields, unhurt.

Yesterday we motored many miles. Where the road was high you looked over immense forests spread out as far as you could see. The spots of red and saffron from the leafy trees on the dark background of the pines, gave them a wild, dangerous look. The men we saw carried guns, generally, and they wore red coats and caps so as not to be mistaken for deer, and shot. We nearly froze though, for the car was open and the top was down.

There's a little boy here named Coster, — the Train's stepson; very polite and quiet. I told him he must read *Smoky*. He's a little bit younger than Janey, but he doesn't know half so much.

I had a letter from Zip which said there was a package for you from Miss Roberts; — but they will have sent it on. A birthday present maybe.

I'm putting in a photograph. You see the island nearest the shore on the left. On the edge of the shore from that, across from a point near its right you can see this house standing up among the trees. Our room is on the furthest side and looks toward the island.

Peg, I think we shall be home early next week.

October 28th, 1926

Darling Pegs: —

Bert has just gone up to bed and I am alone, for Mother has gone to Westport for dinner at the Brookses. I refused to go. I said: I only see my children two hours a day at best and I'm not going to give that little up. So I stayed and after dinner began to read Jane *The Children of the New Forest*, and she liked it; and then I read to Zip and Bert from *War and Peace*. Did you get the book I sent you? I brought Zip a beautiful dummy, — an enormous flat one, to draw in. What are you reading?

Peg, the child who got concussion of the brain is named Weed. I couldn't remember last night. He'll soon be well. I saw Tom Hall this morning on the train and he didn't seem to be bothering his head over the matter. I guess it wasn't really his fault anyway. Mr. Person's, — you know, Barbara Foot's stepfather — has shaved off his moustache and looks the better for it. So has Mr. Clark and so has Mr. Stevenson, and look the worse for it.

Here are Zip and Janey playing a kind of cup and ball game Mother brought home. The ball is like a ping pong ball. The cups are of wire, and each has a snapper that shoots out the ball. One shoots, the other tries to catch. It's good fun.

Mary Ritzo has a dog, a sort of Wee Beastie kind, but larger than Wee Beastie, and white and shaggy. He comes here often though he lives at the Ritzo's. Zippy pets him and begins to wish for Spot.

This is I, going down the hill to the morning Express. I have to hurry but I never miss.

Please write soon.

Your loving Daddy

The summer after we moved to New Canaan, the three older girls and our father all had whooping cough. It was a terrible summer, mainly because he stoically went to work every day in spite of his illness. The two younger girls were sent away. Hence the reference to the Whooping Cough Summer.

October 28th, 1926

Darling Pegs: — Here is Jane listening to *The Children of the New Forest* which I am reading from galley proofs; — for you know we are to publish it in the spring with five full color pictures, like those in *The Black Arrow* and *The Last of the Mohicans.* Janey likes it, but not so well as she did *Smoky.* —

And Zip loves *War and Peace,* even more than Berta did when I read it to her.

I must now read a novel by Mrs. Burt, Julia's mother, which is about the West, and full of 'bad men,' and very exciting. About this kind of man—

Tomorrow is Hallowe'en and both Bert and Zip are to go to parties, — Bert to one at her school, in masks

122   *Father to Daughter*

and fancy dress. She's to be in the Spanish dress Mother got that time she did a Spanish dance in Silvermine in the Whooping Cough Summer. Zip wont tell much about her party because she doesn't want to go; — but she'll probably be glad when she does go. Are you going to a party?

Peg, we've got to go to that old Marshpaug for lunch on Sunday, Mother and I. You remember that rainy day when we drove over in the spring with Mrs. Eaton and Hank. It will mean half the day in a motor even if we don't have a puncture.

Your loving Daddy

October 31, 1926

Darling Pegs: —

This is Berta in the Span-ish dress and the wig she wore to her Halloween party; — but if I had come home be-fore she was dressed I would not have let her go: She went with a bad cough and is now in bed. As soon as she got home we gave her a hot bath, hot lemonade, and asperin and she is doing well.

Zip went to a party at Bar-bara Stearns, but not in fancy dress; — in a fine blue dress though. She didn't get home till ten thirty. And now, though its Sunday, Janey is off for a party at Kitty Stevenson's.

Its raining. The water is dripping from the eaves into the puddles under the windows. We have an enormous log on the fire, — one from the birch tree that died. Zippy is on the bench before the fire-place shaking popcorn, — I can hear it pop. The lights are lighted, though its only three.

I went for a walk this morning before the rain began. I went along the trails in the brown woods, and the trails shone with wet brown leaves. Every puff of wind brought down leaves: they came circling and spiraling down. The sky was melancholy and the woods were grave. I came to that little house where the apple trees grow and found fine red apples; and I sat on a gray rock on the edge of the bluff and ate one, looking out over the brown melancholy tree tops. I had a good rest.

Then I went around the lake. But it began to rain, and I had no hat and my hair was dripping. I ran most of the way. All the trails were soon soaked, and the weeds that grew along them, and my feet and legs got wet. But my suede jacket kept me dry.

Yesterday, Jane, Zip and Mother went with me for a walk. Right near the place where I leave the car, in a field, we found a dead skunk.

November 16th, 1926

Darling Pegs: — This is mother in the kitchen burning Berta's initials into her hockey stick with a red hot skewer. She has to do it on account of a rule of the school. — Peg, poor David Hall has to have his arm broken again, for the third time, and re-set. It has hurt him steadily ever since he fell and he is still in the hospital.

This is Janey in one of her new middie blouses. They are white. On Sunday she and I took a long walk. It was a soft, warm day, like one in June. Jane wore her red hat. We went through the woods to that upland place which is like Scotland and climbed the great rock which is there and sat upon it. There were some black and white cows grazing below us. One had a bell and several wore those long yolks which reach to the ground and prevent them from getting over walls. It was peaceful. We could see the great stretch of bare tree tops, over the rock. Jane dropped her hat, and it fell to the foot of the rock. She went down for it and tried to throw it up; but she could not throw it even a quarter of the way, the rock is so high. Then we ran down the hill and through the sloping meadows and came on home around the lake. Heavy rains have filled up the lake so that it looks much better than even a week ago.

Janey and I on the Rock

Zippy is making beautiful Christmas presents this way: — She buys a box of ginger, a tin box, paints it a smooth black, cuts out a figure of an old fashioned lady in paper, guilds it, and pastes it on the top. It looks like a valuable old-time snuff box of laquer. — I am a great help to her in this for I eat up the ginger.

I expect to come up for you on Thursday night reaching Windsor Friday morning; and to bring you down Saturday night. I hope all the murderers will have been locked up before I arrive.

Your loving Daddy

Father to Daughter

MORE SUMMERS
IN WINDSOR

On the cliffs of Ascutney.

In 1927 Mother's father, Lawrence Saunders (Bopa), who was on a trip to England, was taken seriously ill. After a few days in New York, our parents sailed for England on the Olympic *to be with him. A friend of theirs, Miss Rodman, stayed with us. It was our father's only trip abroad, and he was enormously interested in it. While they were away, we all had chicken pox.*

June 10th, 1927

Darling Berta: — I've sent you a *Boswell's Life*, somewhat abridged. All that is best is in it, and all that is dull is gone. After the first fifty or so pages you will encounter many people you know and like; — and I hope you'll get to like the old Doctor himself. — And if you have to read the book later on in school, why all the better.

Mother is getting a fine rest here, and she looks very well for it. When the train drew out of Windsor she cried; — to the embarrassment of Henry Wardner who caught her at it. He finally said: "Well, I'll withdraw until you are more composed," — which amused and composed her.

You know, until last summer, I only came up to Windsor every two weeks. — And after Friday I shall only be away twice that space of time, if all goes well. And maybe we shall sometime be all back again in New Canaan, and reading aloud beside the fire. I suppose you're all in for chicken pox now, and the Thomases too. Please write me how it goes.

This club is an old gentlman's home, — where beards and whiskers flourish, and the crowns of heads are bare. A horse drawing a baker's wagon just went by — clop, clop, clop, clop — slow and lazy; and looking over this dusky, quiet Victorian room to that old-time sound, and seeing the bearded faces, I went back to long before the war, when leisurable hours were taken leisurely, and women were kept in their places. — I picked up a scientific magazine the other day and read in an article on The Family that in any argument between husband and wife the husband should be regarded as the *umpire,* — which seemed to me neat and conclusive. I couldn't have asked for more than that myself.

Berta, I hope you and the others too, will go to church with Grandma on Sundays. I believe you will like doing it too. You have a deep, religious nature — all people of a deep nature *are* religious truly, even if not technically — and if you can conform to a church it will be best for you and will help to make you happy. Few, if any, can go it alone in this world. And the truest things are known not by the mind but by the feelings. — So do go to church and think about the Service. You'll have plenty of time for pleasure. There's no use to reason about things you know reason can never explain, and if you do it you get a habit of scepticism that enslaves you.

Tonight I just read the ms. of a *History of Mankind,* which is excellently done, and I hope you will sometime read it. But how to publish it is a question — for colleges, or schools, or for the public in general; with pictures or without them? I started the author writing when you were only about five years old by suggesting a book to him which turned out successfully. He's Editor in Chief of the *Herald-Tribune* now. He's been working on this book for years.

Do write again soon, Sweetheart, and write as long a letter as you can.

Your Daddy

Monday, June 13th, 1927

Darling Jenny-Jane: —

This little boy in a red & black striped jacket came to my office to-day to see the Lindbergh parade. He came with Miss Rodman. His name is Sykes. I guess Berta knows him.

Mother came to my office too, but she missed the parade because it was late, and she had to go for an appointment, and I went with her; but she saw the crowd which hid every inch of sidewalk. And at one time the city was in a blizzard of paper which people tore up and threw from all the windows on all the streets; — and when you walk now in places its like walking in dead leaves in the fall, like this.

We came down on the train with Mr. Wardner (Cousin Henry) and ate some of his supper, — a sandwich and a doughnut, both made by his Japanese cook. Poor Mother did not sleep much. — But she got a long nap in the morning in the Hotel where we are. — Mother loves hotels. We just had tea in our room, and gluton bread toasted, and orange marmalade. Mother is taking a nap now.

Here am I telling Miss Rodman about the chicken pox. — And don't any of you kiss her, for she has never had them and says she doesn't want them.

I hope you and the girlies will write; and if anyone does it before Thursday, why send the letter to my office: — c/o Scribner's, 597 Fifth Ave.

Tell Zip I'm sorry she's got the chicks; — but she'll be the second one to get well; and give Berta the paper I enclose about Montaigne.

Your loving Daddy

While they were in New York, preparing to leave for London, they received a letter of introduction to James Barrie, the author of Peter Pan, *who lived in London.*

Tuesday, June 14th, 1927

Darling Zippy: —
This is a drippy day. The streets are puddled and the wheels of the taxis are reflected in the shining asphalt, and if Mother were not here I would be so unhappy I do not believe I could write you a letter.

Mother is having a splendid rest, staying late a'bed. Her cold is gone and she looks well. We ought to see Barrie in London. We have a letter introducing us. Mother thinks that alone is worth the trip, but I'd rather look upon old mother Ascutney any day, — not to mention Bertha, Elizabeth, Peggy and Jane.

How are your chicken pocks? When I had it I was in the top floor of the Infirmary alone; and the walk to the big play ground passed the infirmary. It was fall, and the Third Isthmean Foot Ball Team, of which I was quarter back, and Captain, went by in a group, and they saw me and gave me three Cheers and tried to throw the football up to my window. — A nurse ran out and stopped them. The ball might carry the pocks. — But I had distributed them already, and soon after I was released many others were imprisoned.

You must write soon Zippy. Tell me how your lessons with Aunt Molly go, and how you all are. Is Berta reading Boswell's *Life of Johnson*? I'm going to enter you for the Wickham-Rise School tomorrow. Bert is already entered. — But I'm glad you are not going for a year.

Now I must walk back to Mother in the rain.

Your Daddy

June 18th, 12:10 A.M.

Darling Zippy: —

I was sitting with Mother on the deck, waiting for the boat to sail and wondering whether I had enough money to bribe the Captain to sail it up the Connecticut River, when along came Mr. T. Ellsworth. He monopolized the conversation and so I said: "if I can't talk to Mother, I'll talk to Zip even if I have nothing to say but thank you and Mlle. and the others for the flowers." We found them in our state room which has a big round porthole in it and two very narrow beds across from each other. Edwin drove us to the boat, with all our bags which I had thought Mother never would get packed. First we went to Bopa's and saw Jocko and the Parrot who seemed very lonely; and Mr. Heydon came with us to the dock. After a while along came Aunt Jean and Uncle Jack. They say Bill now does very well in his studies. — But now they have gone, and all the other people who are not passengers are going, — and soon *we* shall be going, — and I hope I'll never have to do it again without at least some of my children.

A steward is now going about beating on a gong and calling "All visitors on shore please." I wonder if I could fool him into thinking I was a Visitor. — And the ship is shaking, so they must have started the engines, — although I think little tug boats pull us out.

Please write us very soon darling. I'm sorry you had chicken-pox so badly, — but now the worst of it must be over.

Your loving Daddy

June 20th, 1927

Darling Jenny-Jane: —

This is Mother in her deck chair, all tucked in with a blanket. There is a steward who does nothing but tuck people in. He has brass buttons on his blue coat.

Jen; I wanted to find out if I would be seasick, but how can I? — Its like crossing the Hudson River in a ferry boat. Besides, I'm so sleepy all the time that if I even lie in a deck chair, I go right to sleep.

This is the best way to see the water: — look out of your porthole which is about twenty feet above it. The waves the ship makes are like the surf on a beach and the spray from them wets your face. In the next stateroom to ours are some children. — We hear them every morning. The little girl sings to her doll: "Baby came from Heaven;" — or maybe she sings it to the real baby that is in there. Two little girls about the ages of Peggy and Zip have deck chairs next to ours, with their Aunt or Grandmother. They have a dog.

There are other children on the boat too, but the children who really have fun are the very poor ones whose mothers wear shawls over their heads. They have the very best deck on the ship and we're not allowed to go there. — It is at the stern end, so they can look back along the foamy green track the ship makes in the blue sea. There are swings and trapezes and lots of other children in ragged shirts and trousers. — So, if we ever all go abroad, I'll put on a flannel shirt and corduroy trousers and mother will wear a shawl over her head, and we'll go as very poor people and really have fun.

Your loving Daddy

June 21st, 1927

Darling Pegs: —
Now we're over halfway to England and we've had nothing but sunshine and calm seas. The ship is rolling the least bit now — I can feel my weight shift Slowly from my right elbow to my left — and it pitched the least bit a couple of days ago; but not enough to find out whether or not you would be seasick. I've been hoping for a storm but there's no prospect of one. — Maybe there will be one when we come back. The ocean looks almost like the pond in Windsor on a very windy day, only that there is nothing *but* ocean. We saw yesterday a schooner with three masts far off — her sails and hull were the whitest white on the dark blue wrinkled ground of the ocean. We passed some sail ships on the second day, very near us, and they looked tiny from the deck of this big ship. There's very little to do but walk up and down and you feel sleepy all the time. — I could lie down and go to sleep now, but I think I'll get my overcoat and go to the top deck under the stars and walk up and down, alone, and think of my girlies in Windsor.

There's one good game they play on the upper deck, and if you and Zippy were here I would play it with you. There is a net, like that in Badminton and a court is marked off like a tennis court, but very small. But you have no ball or racket, but a rubber ring; — that you throw the instant you catch it, and you must catch it in one hand. You serve and return just as in tennis. Those two little girls I wrote Janey about — the daughters of Secritary Davis, of the navy — play it all the time.

We're more than halfway to England now. We'll see France two days from now when we stop early at Cherbourg. That night we get to Southampton.

A week later you will get this letter and three weeks after that (I hope) we'll be home.

Your loving daddy

June 25th, 1927

Darling Berta: —
If I was a little disappointed in the Atlantic I was not in London which we have been going about all day; — This afternoon in a motor with Bopa who, though feeble, is very much himself. Our plan is to sail on July 2nd on the *Aquatania.* — Passage is engaged. We ought therefore to be in Windsor, which even now I hold over London, about a week after you get this. We shall be here for just one week.

London is altogether different from New York. The houses are real houses, low and homelike; and there are many little lawns and gardens, and trees that are richer and fuller than ours, even in the country; and there are many squares with parks of trees in the centers, or with simple, noble monuments, — great shafts with statues around the bases and on the tops. Many of the residential parts are exactly like you would know, from Thackeray, and the business parts are varied in style and color; and everyone seems polite and friendly.

We saw the sentries before Buckingham Palace in scarlet coats and bearskin hats, standing like painted statues, with bayonettes fixed; and as we stopped beside the great bank of England, which has not a window in it, the guard marched up, — a platoon of redcoated grenadiers, the officer with drawn sword — and marched through the arched door which closed behind them.

We saw the Town of London, a mediaeval castle, with a moat: — great square towers, sheer gray walls of masonry, and battlements with loopholes in the shape of crosses. We drove all around it, and saw in the front, on the embankment the iron doors of the traitor's gate.

We stopped at the little alley, wide enough for one man to pass another, which leads into the Cheshire Cheese, — and we entered in the footsteps of Dr Johnson, Garrick; Goldsmith, Burke and Reynolds. There was sand on the floors and the panelled woodwork was black. The little square panes in the windows were bubbled. We saw the wooden chair — all black with age — that Johnson used to sit in and deliver the law. Then we went down — and I bumped my head on the low ceiling — into the stone walled, arched-roofed wine cellars which had been part of an ancient monastery.

And all the time I was wishing you were here, for it was all exactly after your heart. I hope I may see it with you someday. — But almost the best sight of all is that from Bopa's windows of the Thames flowing between its borders of trees, bearing up barges and tugs, under its many arched bridges. The great buildings of Parliament are also visible from that window, and the fine high tower that contains Big Ben.

I hope you have all written us, darling; but, anyway, there will be no use in you doing it after this reaches you.

Your loving daddy,

Maxwell E. Perkins

Jane came of age just at the start of World War II. After the war she married a British naval officer and went to England to live. She loved England and was very happy there. How her father would have loved to visit her there in her thatched-roof farmhouse in Dorset! But she didn't marry until after his death.

Before her marriage, Jane was doing well as an editor in New York. He was very pleased about this and proud of her.

Tuesday, June 28th, 1927

Darling, darling Janey, —
Yesterday, coming from the Galsworthy's, where we were at lunch, we saw some little English girls dressed like this, in blue coats. They were so like you girls, Janey! It made me homesick for you all. — But that I am all the time, and if Bopa and Mother were not here I believe I'd jump off Waterloo Bridge into the Thames River.

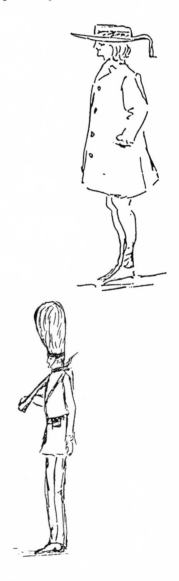

Janey; you see a good many soldiers in London, standing as sentries before the palaces and The Tower, and they are like the soldiers of a hundred years ago. They wear the coats that gave them the name of "The Red Coats" in the American Revolution. You should see the sheen of their bayonets when they march.

On Sunday, Mother and I went to tea in Richmond which is near London, in what they call the Old Palace; — for the walls and towers

Father to Daughter

are those of a palace where Queen Elizabeth used to stay, and where she died. But the inside has been made over into modern rooms.

Now the room where she died of a broken heart is over a gateway that we drove through. And under the casement she had been looking through is a coat of arms in stone, — such very old, old stone.

Today we got our first letters in England — two from Zippy and one from Peg. — Poor Zip! What a bad time she had. I hope more letters will come in a day or two.

On Sunday the Galsworthy's are going to drive us out to their country house in Sussex. We'll see English villages and English country. — Give the letter from Barrie that I put in to Bert. She can paste it in her scrap book.

Your loving daddie
Maxwell Perkins

We put off our sailing to a week from tomorrow. Our boat is the Majestic.

Daddie

Here we are having tea in the train coming up to London. You are in a little compartment just like a fine old stage coach in shape, with green brocaded seats. — Much more fun than our trains.

Daddy

More Summers in Windsor

Thursday, July 7th, 1927

Darling Zippy: —
This is the biggest ship afloat, and I can see, we wont get a
roll or a pitch out of her, though the sea is spotted with
foam. When we left Southampton yesterday we saw once
more a splendid old castle of Edward VIths time on a green
lawn with cows grazing on it. — A real castle, ivy covered,
exactly as it was hundreds of years ago.

Mother saw the Prince of Wales in a procession. He was
sitting beside the King of Egypt in a carriage with postillions
in scarlet livery. I saw the procession from a distance. Horse
guards in shining steel breast plates and helmets, with
drawn sabers, thundered along, before and behind, on big
black horses. They had scarlet sleeves and white trousers
and black boots. One time we saw the baby of the Duchess
of York and her princess cousin driving in a brougham.
Each princess was in the lap of a nurse in a gray uniform
and a cap with ribbons. On the door of the brougham was
painted a coronet.

We went to the house of Commons and saw Parliament.
The hall where it sits is shaped like a church. The members
sit on benches like pews, but instead of running crosswise,
they run lengthwise. Those of one party sit on one side and

those of the other opposite. Winston Churchill, whom I someday hope to persuade to write a history of the British Empire, made a speech, and whenever he said anything the members of either party liked, they would say "Hear! Hear!" Some of the members wore high hats, and kept them on. The speaker wore a white wig with a queue, and sat at an end on a kind of throne. Mother said it reminded her of Alice in Wonderland.

But, Zip; — the trouble with England is that the rain falls all the time. We have had only *one* sunny day, and even then there were many clouds in the sky. — But that makes the trees very full and green; and everywhere in London you run upon squares that are like tropical gardens. — If it weren't for the rain, London would be much better than New York.

This is an English school girl. They all wear a kind of dark blue uniform, — coat, hat, skirt, all dark blue.

Your loving Daddy
Maxwell Perkins

Thursday, July 7th, 1927

Darling Pegs:

We had a walk on the Downs, in Sussex, and I picked up a piece of chalk that I'm bringing home. John Galsworthy took us down there to his house in his motor. We went through many English villages with winding streets that climbed up and down hills and we saw thatched cottages, and slow, full rivers, like big quiet brooks; — but the downs were best of all. They are long, high hills, green and bare, with springy soil. You walk along their tops and look out forever over the dark green country with the heavy clumps of trees, and the regular fields marked off with fences. The colors are deeper and calmer than those of American country, and the buildings are so moss grown and grass grown that they sink into the landscape. There, on the downs, was when we most wished we had you children with us.

I was disappointed when we woke in the morning, for I knew a maid would walk right in and wake us, and I thought she would bring tea. But Mother had told Mrs. Sauter, Galsworthy's niece, that we would rather have fruit. — So we sat up in bed and ate raspberries, which seemed silly.

At breakfast, you are not waited on. Everything is put on a side table and you go and get it yourself. — And they have so much. — fruit, cereal, bacon, eggs, mushrooms, coffee, muffins, and Gammon. Do you know what Gammon is? — A kind of ham. Remember Gammon and Spinach? Mother ate some, but I had already eaten so much more than usual that I couldn't.

Mr. Sauter is an artist and he took a fancy to *my head.* He thought I had a much better head than anyone else ever thought I had. He said he wanted to *do* it, — which made me nervous and I changed the subject. But when we got back to the hotel Mother got ambitious to have him do it, and we had an awful time. She called him up, and in he came; —

Father to Daughter

but we had little time, and it wasn't a success. — To sit and have your head *done* is worse than going to a dentist.

Then I called upon Lady Cynthia Asquith who wrote that story about the English boy and the burgular. She is quite a grand lady and you call her "Lady Cynthia." I told her how you all liked her book and she tried to find a copy to write in for you, but she had none. She was quite pretty, and simple, and I thought her shy; — but Mother says I always think people shy when they don't like me.* She was like a Boston lady and I thought her very nice whether she was shy or not. She had a chow like Wang who followed me down stairs in a murderous way, but let me go safely in the end.

Your loving Daddy
Maxwell Perkins

*I never said that. Everybody likes Daddy. *L.S.P.*

July 14th, 1927

Darling Pegs: —

I hope you are having better weather than we. — Clouds, drizzle, rain, drizzle, all the week. Almost as bad as London! I guess all the good weather is over the ocean, where it ought to be bad.

Tell Berta I've sent her a novel by Charles Kingsley, about Alexandria when it was the greatest city and place in the world. Its name is *Hypatia,* — a lady who lived there. Tell Zip I've entered her in the Wickham-Rise; — so she must study hard with Aunt Molly.

This is a man who just came up — a very grand and great man. I kept my eyes on my paper, pretending not to see him, but up he came. He dresses beautifully and has beautiful manners, and we're to have dinner together unless I'm

mighty smart about excuses. If you marry such a man you'll have a town and country house, and a Rolls Royce, and a maid, and for a husband an

And I won't ask you to come see me in my cabin on Pasture Hill.

Pegs, I hate this city and every one of the million billion stones it is made of. The trouble is I've put all my eggs in one basket, the whole six of them, and that basket is the Edminster House, North Main Street, Windsor, Vermont.

Your loving daddy
Maxwell Perkins

Father to Daughter

August 1, 1927

Darling Jenny-Jane: —

This is Zippy's day for a letter but I'm writing to you out of turn because tomorrow is your birthday and you're seven years old. This day last year you couldn't swim and you couldn't read to yourself. Now you swim well and you're as great a reader as any of them. You love good books too.

I remember so well when first I heard your voice. I was on the stairs in the Plainfield house early in the morning and the war was going on, and the voice came from

Mother's room. — It was a baby's cry! I said to myself "That's the cry of a boy baby. God sent me a boy to make up for my not going to the war." And I was sorry when I found it was a girl: — but that was because I didn't know it was 'You.' There never had been a 'You' in the world before, and so how could I know how lucky I was. Like Berta, I didn't know who it was or what it was. If I'd known it was 'You' and what 'You' were, I wouldn't have thought about any boys.

Here we are at Southern Pines looking at the snake.

Goodbye Janey — I wish I could kiss you ten times tomorrow. You've been a good girl for seven years, and I believe you will be good for all your years and make people happy.

Your loving daddy,
Maxwell Perkins

Father to Daughter

August 9th, 1927

Dearest Peg: —

I've just been having lunch with a lady who admires Mother, — Eleanor Tweed. We talked about Windsor, and all the people there. Now she wants me to go to her apartment at six and have a cocktail; — and you know I hate cocktails. I don't want to go and I don't believe I shall.

Did Jane like the letter about Ohl's Pond? You could catch turtles there from the bank, for they would poke their heads up through the weeds and you would grab just behind the head and get the turtle. One day we were all doing this. Uncle Edward was looking sharply for a head. He saw one and grabbed, — and brought out a long slimey snake! You know a snake's head is almost exactly like a turtles.

Oh, Pegs, Mr. Hamilton wrote me that our cat has had *seven* new kittens! Now whats to be done about all these cats when the Hamiliton's leave the house?

Your loving daddy
Maxwell Perkins

August 21st, 1927

Darling Zippy: —

I'll tell the story of how we arrested the King of the Blackhand. That was a society of blackmailers and murderers, Italians, when I was a reporter on the *Times*. One night at about one o'clock I finished a story and put on my hat to go home. As I got up, the night city editor came running across the city room.

"Perkins" said he, "here's a story I'd like to cover myself. Detective Kirby has just called up — "

And then he went on to tell me of a plan to arrest the King of the Black Hand who was in hiding among a gang of laborers in Mt. Kisco. Well, it was my style of story too and I followed directions carefully.

Father to Daughter

I got on the two o'clock train and walked through from the front, armed with a heavy cane I had borrowed from the Harvard Club, and when I saw a man with a black moustache and a red tie sitting with another man I stopped, took out my handkerchief, and blew my nose. Instantly he took off his hat and pushed it back and I walked on and sat down some seats behind: — for I knew he was detective Kirby.

At Mt. Kisco in the dark, I went up to him and shook hands. "Have you got a gun," he said. "We may have trouble." "I've got a good stick" I said. A local policeman joined us and off we went in the dark, stumbling along a frozen road.

Finally, we saw black shapes rise up. — Sheds, they were, and one flimsy house. Kirby knocked at the house door. A frightened woman's voice came from a window.

"Who's there"?

"Never mind who" said Kirby.

"Down you come and open the door or we'll kick it in."

She opened. The detectives entered with drawn pistols and I with my stick. The woman sobbed and shivered in a red kimono by the lantern light. Kirby bullied her while the others searched and found no one. — And he learned from her what he wanted.

We went out into the dark and forced open a long shed. There were many dim beds in a row and men upon them.

The detectives held their guns pointed. Kirby took the lantern and held it in the face of the third man. He woke, rose up quickly, jabbered Italian. Others rose up but the guns were trained on them. Kirby caught his man by the collar and dragged him out the door.

As we walked away in the dark, I had a shivery feeling up and down my back. What if one of those men took a shot at us? But no one did. They knew Kirby. We tramped the frozen road with the prisoner in hand cuffs and listened for a time to the wails of the woman.

Your loving daddy
Maxwell Perkins

At this time, Bert was waiting for word from the Chapin School to go down for an interview with Miss Chapin. She passed and spent her last two years of high school at Chapin.

August 21st, 1927

Darling Berta:
No word from Miss Chapin. — I guess you won't be needed this week, anyway, though I've bought chairs on the Friday

train for you and mother.

An old friend came in today, — from Papeete, Tahiti, in the South Seas. Frank Stimson. He and the Brooks boys and we formed an inseparable group from the ages of seven or eight upward to boarding school and college. He was always brilliant, and always failed because of his eccentricities, and finally drifted to the South Seas where most go to the devil. — But here he is, impressively stout, with a moustache and the ghost of a goatee, and the reputation of a great scholar; — for, just for the fun of the thing, which was always his only reason, he has made a dictionary and a grammar of the language of those islands, which was never done before and has greatly excited all the philologists and anthropologists, etc. — Henceforth, for a museum in Honolulu, he is to sail from island to island, and study native traditions and histories, etc., and sometimes come back here to lecture at universities (I don't think he even got his AB) before bodies of scholars. It's always grand to see someone who just did as he pleased and came through. He did because he had from birth both energy and intellect. He looked something like

this. He was a great boy and he's the same person now because he's always been his own self. The public be hanged!

The Perkins boys, Edward, Max and Charlie, were considered "wild," and the McClarys didn't like their children to associate with them. To judge by the contents of this letter, their fears were justified. Typically, Max took full responsibility for the accident. However, Bert met Tom McClary many years later and he said, "You're Max's daughter? Your father saved my life when I was a boy."

August 24th, 1927

Darling Berta: — You must show this letter to Janey for it's the story of how I nearly killed Tom McClary.

You can see him any day in Windsor now, long and boney, walking with stooped-shoulders and bent knees, looking sorrowful. — Or peering out shyly through the bars in the cashiers window in his bank. But when he was a boy, I went swimming with him in a deep pool way up the Blow me down pond, though he couldnt swim.

We should have had no trouble if we hadn't thought the other side of the pond was better. But we wanted to go there and I said I would swim him over if he would rest his hands lightly on my shoulders. — So, off we started.

Father to Daughter

We were going smoothly, half way across, when Tom, somehow, lost his nerve, threw his arms around my neck, and clung to me. We sank. I struggled. I twisted and tried to turn round to fight him off. No use. He held me with all his might. I had to open my mouth and in poured the water. I thought this fool has drowned us. I could not swim up. I was furious with Tom. Just then he let me loose. He had swallowed more water than I and was almost done. I came up like a cork, felt instantly right, and started for shore. Then I thought of Tom and looked over my shoulder. He was

floating, limp, his face down, three feet under water. I reached down, caught his wrist, and towed him ashore. In order to lift him up the bank I joined my hands under his stomach and gave him a heave and water poured from his mouth. I thought he was dead, but in a minute I saw he was gasping and very soon he was quite right again. — By pure luck, I had done just the right thing by lifting him under his stomach: that made the water come out.

We rode home on our bicycles, very quiet and agreed to say nothing of the adventure. — But I told Grandma under promise of secrecy.

Berta, are you having the hay fever. It struck me at noon and I've done some first class sneezing.

Your loving daddy
Maxwell Perkins

September 1, 1927

Darling Peg: — It was this way at breakfast today, for a friend of Uncle Louis spent the night and he too had hay fever. In fact, Uncle Louis woke us all up by his sneezes so we had lots of time.

Last night I dined here with Uncle Edward and then walked home with him, and he talked about Louie. Do you remember her? Zipper does. She was at Windsor.

Uncle Louis just went out of this club with his friend, one of the tallest men in the world. This is the way they looked.

This tall man was too tall for the American Army in the war so he went into the English Army. A Scotch regiment that wore kilts; — and they had to sew one kilt by the top to the bottom of another in order to cover him to the knees.

Your Daddy

Father to Daughter

September 7th, 1927

Dearest Bert: — I'm so glad you were in the play and that you did your parts so beautifully. I had seen the others before. I knew how well they could do; — but you had hidden that particular light of yours under a bushel, — and how brightly it shone when you uncovered it!

Now I'll tell you a story, though you've heard it many times, of how Edward and I met General Sherman when I was about five years old.

We were visiting at Grandpa Evartses — then Senator for N.Y. — in Washington. One day, we two were in the drawing room. The door bell rang! Someone came toward the door. We scuttled under the table, a tall thin man entered. — We

lay low, but could not forbear from giggling as Aunt Mary came in with Sherman. She and the General looked in surprise at the table. We giggled some more. Aunt Mary said: "Oh, those are Betty's boys. Come out boys; this is General Sherman." We giggled some more. Said Sherman in a deep voice: "You boys come right out now or I'll get some of my big guns and blow you out." And out we came giggling, as he told Aunt Mary of some very big cannon they had just had made for the Army.

So, I remember well shaking hands with a tall, thin man with a white pin-feathery beard. — And that was the Great General who marched through Georgia, and said "War is Hell!"

Your loving daddy, Maxwell E. Perkins

June 19th, 1928

Darling Pegs: — Your Mother has learned to manipulate the radio, — which makes me more than ever opposed to our having one. First Bopa goes and tinkers with it to make it louder; then Mother goes to make it lower; then Bopa tries

Father to Daughter

to improve on that, and then Mother. Some night there will be three murders by drowning at 246 E 49th. The place: my bathtub; the victims: one monkey, one parrot, one radio, the guilty one, myself, — and with a light conscience at that.

It's this kind of day here, — Pour and drip, drip and pour. Let us pray for a drought in July. But Mother likes it. She spends her time at movies and theaters.

Here we are at dinner. We can't talk much because Polly and the radio want to; — and the monkey helps them along by scolding upstairs. — But I'm going now to the Grand Central to buy railroad tickets for Windsor for Friday night.

Your loving Daddy,
Maxwell E. Perkins

More Summers in Windsor 157

June 20th, 1928

Darling Janey: —

Mother and I and Auntie Margaret went to the theatre last night; — but the play was rather silly, I thought. There was a burglar in it, with a flashlight. Here we are in the lobby. See

the umbrellas. Soon we'll carry umbrellas as they do in London, all the time; and always turn our trousers up. — That custom came from England, and when first followed here, when this was a sunny land, the fresh little boys used to call out to the dudes — "Hey Mister! Is it rainin' in London?" That was in the Nineties.

Tell Berta I've got for her a copy of *The Danvers' Jewels* and I will bring it up on Friday night. I have the railroad tickets for mother and myself. I think she will come on my train.

Your loving daddy,
Maxwell E. Perkins

Father to Daughter

Though our father wrote to the four older girls in turn, so that we should all have more or less the same number of letters, many have been lost. Of the letters that survived, Bert and Peggy have the most and Jane only a few. Nancy, born in 1925, didn't get as many letters as her sisters; only one letter and a poem have survived.

When she was a very little girl, she wouldn't kiss her Daddy because he was "too prickly."

June 26th, 1928

Darling Nancy: — Here you are in bed, and poor daddy, who has to go back to horrible New York, is begging for a kiss. Won't you send him one in a letter.

Nance, in New York there is no grass for the children to play on. So they play right in the street. They play ball, and I see them when I go home to Bopas at night. Here are two of them. When motors come they have to jump out of the way. Aren't you sorry for them?

Have you seen the baby cow today? Are his legs still wobbly? You never see any cows, dogs, or horses in New York, — only automobiles everywhere.

This is what I must go and do now: — Get my hair cut. Then when I come to Windsor I will look so very nice that you may be willing to kiss me. Will you?

Father to Daughter

Here is Nancy in the new boat that is coming to Windsor
for her.

Your loving daddy,
Maxwell E. Perkins

Peggy kept a diary for almost a year when she was thirteen. She told this story of the cat in her entries for June 1 and 2, 1929.

Oh what happened last night or at least at about 2 this morning!!! In the night Jane came into my room and said, "Peggy, there's somebody in the bathroom. And I heard somebody cry out!" I heard it too but alas! I didn't go in but thought the cry was only some Italian child and the sounds only the house creaking. But later on I heard some thing on the roof and it jumped into my room! Then I heard it jump into Zippy's room. I was scared and I got up and went in. The light from my room shone in and there was the big cat sitting and looking stealthily at Zippy. She woke up just as I pointed at the cat and cried out. When I pointed he sprung out the window. Zippy said to go and look at the baby cat. I went and there she lay, dead, with her poor little neck all bloody! The cruel stealthy sneaky cat had murdered her in the dark!! We didn't want Jane or Nancy to see her so we took her out and buried her.

Sunday June 2

Yes, we took her out and buried her in the night. We opened the cellar door and took Toby with us and he seemed so honest and kind. When we came back there was the cat smelling the place where the kitty had lain! When he saw us he knew he was trapped so he gave a pitiful little miow! The artful, sly, bloodthirsty Cat! We all but broke his sneaky backbone! Poor pretty Miss Flora that we'd only had three days! He killed our birdy and he killed our kitty!

Father to Daughter

July 18th, [1929]

Darling Peg: —

Lots of people have tried to finish *Edwin Drood,* and some of
the endings have been published. Some think it Dickens'
best book, — but that's always said of a writer's unfinished
book just as it's said of an unfinished life: the boy who died
young was always 'the best of the lot'. Have you done another composition? If you do the one about the cat, will you
send it to me? That cat was Evil! The older people, with
senses blunted by reason, didn't realize it, but the children
knew it, — they felt it. The youngest the most. And don't
forget to put in the burial. Think it all over and feel it before
you write it.

Peg, I've always thought that a barred cell had advan-
tages over a hotel bed-room. Now I'm sure of it. For one
thing the cell would be cooler and it wouldn't have pale
green walls. — But where else can I go? If only you were

here all would be right enough. The only cell I ever stayed in was quite interesting. There was a barred window and by standing tip toe on the wooden bunk I could easily reach the bars. I pulled at them, but they were not loose and I had no file, so my only chance to make an escape was lost. — Besides, I reflected, I couldn't leave Walter who was in the next cell making melancholy attempts to sing "See the Little Elis". But then they put in with me a tramp and a negro, both dispirited. — We sat in a row on the bunk and smoked up my cigarettes and spoke disrespectfully of the police of the City of Boston, — that is, the tramp and I did. The negro acquiesced with half hearted chuckles.

When we got out — Walter and I, bailed by friends, the dawn was coming, and we all ate a magnificent meal of buckwheat cakes at a lunch counter. But wasn't it decent of those other fellows to sit up all night to get us out of gaol? I wish such friends would come and bail me out of this hotel. — Really, I have "friends" in Baltimore, if I chose to look them up.

Your loving daddy
Maxwell Perkins

Father to Daughter

VALENTINES
AND SONGS

We found these illustrated poems on our plates on the breakfast table when we came down on Valentine's Day, after our father had left for the train. They are perfectly suited to the child for whom they were intended and have caught that child forever as a small portrait might do. Looking back over the years at these valentines, my sister Peg and I realized that they are quite unique.

I have seven valentines written consecutively over a period of seven years. Somehow all of mine have been preserved. Zippy, two years younger than I, must have had at least five, but only one has survived. Peg, again two years younger, has three, probably the complete set. Jane, younger still, had only one, but this is probably right for her. Nance came along too late to have any.

Father to Daughter

To My Valentine

Through all the golden summer time
    We walk the hills together;
And when the icy winter blows
    To heap the hills with drifted snows
We seek that golden land of books
    Where there is Summer weather –

So be it rough or be it fine
    Please always be my Valentine

To Bertha

My love she loves a knight at arms
    Who charged a thousand years ago.
My love she loves a sailor bold
    Who cruised to Westward Ho!
My love she loves a highland chief
    Who would not to proud Edward yield.
—Against such mighty ones, in grief,
    I needs must leave the field.

Knight of the Leopard, Amyas Leigh,
    And Wallace, heroes though ye were,
Ye'er false to vows of chivalry,
    Proclaimed in lands from palm to fir,
That ye should steal a maiden's love
    From him who made ye known to her.

Leopard, ye were to Edith true!
    And Leigh, ye knew the loss of Rose!
Wallace, fair Marion died for you!
    —Berta, I love as ye loved those.
Come! Stand aside! Give me my due,
    Leave me the Valentine I chose.

To Bert

Our days are not as other days
When Arthur dwelt at Camelot –
Then if by chance I'd meet a knight
He'd hew my head off like as not –
Yet if you'll be my Guinevere,
I'll gladly be your Lancelot.

Near Nothingham, t'was dangerous where,
Roamed merry men in fair greenwood,
The sheriff might well catch me there
And hang me high for black crow's food.
But I will be your Little John
If you will be my Robin Hood.

In spacious days of Charlemagne
The beasts on men were prone to dine:
I don't like bears and wolves and boars!
And hairy Ogres! not for mine!
But I will be your Orson rough,
If you'll but be my Valentine.

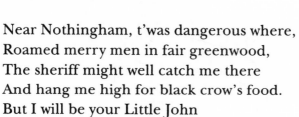

To Zipper

Who is this maid of royal mein
    Who lightly treads on slender feet,
Her graceful figure dimly seen
Beneath a gown all fresh and neat.
    Her little face, her eyes of green
        Seem only to some princess meet.

But then I've seen her like a boy,
    Eager to romp, or coast, or skate,
In knickers of rough corduroy
Stride onward with a rowdy gait
    All outdoors anxious to enjoy,
        Adventurous for any fate.

170   *Father to Daughter*

Hers is the charm of glamorous maid,
    The boylike enterprise of youth,
Within the house a lady staid
Quick to gaiety or ruth;
    Without alert and unafraid
        A rough and ready boy in truth.

Just such a one as I'd design
    To make a perfect Valentine.

Valentines and Songs

Father to Daughter

To Peggy

"Where is Peggy?"
She's abroad, on adventure bent
Searching some brook for its source
    Till day's light is spent
She would sail with Amyas
    To a new world's rim,
Or cut a path with Stanley
    Into the jungle dim.

"Where's Peggy?"
Now it's dark she is hid away,
Reading in some secret nook
    Of a bloody fray
When the lean young Bonaparte
    Poured his armies out
Upon the plains of Lombardy
    The Austrians to rout.

"Where's Peggy?"
Will she take me exploring too?
I would trace the twisting brook
    All the long day through.
I with Bonaparte would march
    Or face the ocean's brine
Peggy answer! Pity give
    And be my Valentine.

To Peggy

Gentle maid of bearing nice
Softly going thy own ways,
Asking no help or advice,
Busy through the longest days,
Till you show something you've wrought
With hands only *you* have taught.

Silent, strangers being by,
You watch with quaint countenance,
Catching with quick merry eye
Every move's significance.
Questioned you've an answer shrewd
For with humor you're endued.

Charm and talent all compact
Thou was't made admired to be.
Quick to grasp and swift to act
Free me from my misery —
Grant me this one boon at last!
Only thou the power has't.

What ask *I* of one so rare,
Wise, discreet and self contained?
Plainly, that you truly care
For me, wretched, till I've gained
Thy love; — briefly, lady fine,
That you'll be my Valentine.

TO MY VALELENTINE

To Janey

There was a maiden loved me—
    Oh that was long ago!
We tramped the hills together—
    O, that we still did so.
And of a Sunday morning, howe'er
    the day might be,
We'd search the shaggy mountain sides
    The sprightly goats to see.

She rode upon my shoulders then—
    Ah, but she rides no more!
For she has learned to skip, and hop,
    and bound about the floor.
The sprightly goats she's quite forgot,
    To me she pays no heed,
For of my mighty shoulders now
    She has no further need.

        Father to Daughter

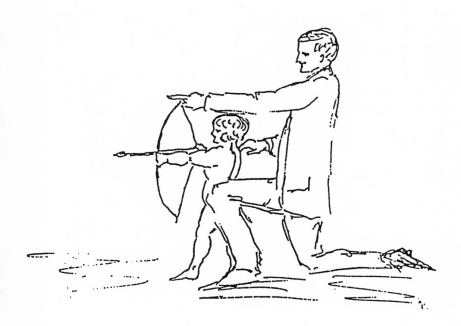

Alone I stride the mountains
    in sunlight and in rain:
Alone I climb the rocky trails
    I used to climb with Jane!
The goats now gaze upon me
    With eyes of sad reproof:
They shake their horns in sorrow,
    They point a scornful hoof.

So little cupid hear me:—
    This day this prayer I make,
Not only for my lonely self, but
    for a poor goat's sake—
Shoot at the heart of Janey
    An arrow keen and fine
So that she may at last consent
    To be my Valentine.

Valentines and Songs

To Peg

I sit among dark shadows in a stately
    house of gloom.
Grave portraits stare with a frowning air
    from the carved walls of the room.

But a landscapes bright in the golden light
    and the wind flows clean and free
and love abides on the fair hillsides
    of the land where I should be.

I tramp down stone paved channels
    where the taxies grind and lurch
You glimpse on the edge of forests deep
    the flash of the sun touched birch.
I watch the bleak stone buildings
    while the motors grate and whine.
You see on the distant hillside
    the grand and ragged pine.

I must talk of proofs and copyright
    and libel laws and bills
To stiff legged men who would never ken
    the peace of the Cornish hills;
While you with Zip and Jane and Bert
    your fill of pleasure take
When you go for a swim at the grassy rim
    of the smooth and shining lake.

           * * *

This being the case, oughtn't you to write me
a nice long letter?

Daddy

Father to Daughter

In 1934, when Nancy was nine, the family was scattered. Nobody was in Windsor. This song was written to Nancy in New Canaan, and was probably the last letter he illustrated for any of his children.

Old Zippy's in Wyoming
    A'riding the prair-ee
And Peggy as a cow-girl
    Is happy as can be
But Daddy's in his office
    And that's as bad as school
They all have it easy but
    The Old Gray Mule

The Old Gray Mule
    Isn't he the fool!
They all have it easy but
    The Old Gray Mule

Now Nancy's in New Canaan
    And plays all day with Kim,
And Janey's at the Holmwood
    And daily has a swim,
But Daddy's at the office
    And how can he keep cool?
They all have it easy but
    The Old Gray Mule

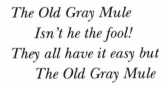

CHARLES SCRIBNER'S SONS
PUBLISHERS - IMPORTERS - BOOKSELLERS
597 FIFTH AVENUE
NEW YORK

The Old Gray Mule
Isn't he the fool!
They all have it easy but
The Old Gray Mule

They sail down to Bermuda
Upon the rolling tide.
And then at Old Point Comfort
They swim and walk and ride
But you'll find Dad in his office
And working, as a rule.
They all have it easy but
The Old Gray Mule

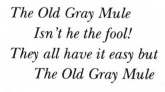

The Old Gray Mule
Isn't he the fool!
They all have it easy but
The Old Gray Mule

Father to Daughter

BERT'S TRIP

*In 1928 Bert was taken out of school to accompany her Grand-
mother Perkins on a Mediterranean cruise. The grown-ups must
have thought that the trip would be a more valuable experience
than school. Because Bert was sixteen and had never been away
from home on her own before, our father knew she would be homesick and wrote a long letter to every port of call, doing his best to
give her the feel of home, which Peg expressed so well in her diary.*

*"When we came home from the beach I was overwhelmed by a
feeling of love and comfort for this dear old house. And the
curve of the bay windows from the diningroom looked so
busumy! Every inch of it has been made homelike by my family.
And though we're all different, we're all Maxwell Perkinses!"*

(Peggy's diary, June 23, 1929)

January 22, 1928

My darling Berta: —
I'll write you a letter every day to the day of mailing and
generally I'll do it at night, in bed; — but this being Sunday
I'm writing at Mother's desk. Its a very cold day, and still. Dr.
Jimenes' pines go up straight and motionless except at the
tops where they wave a little against the blue sky. The two
church steeples are bright in the sun and the white walls of
the Norman farmhouse shine in it.

Zippy and Jane are playing "the Game" in the dining
room. — I hear an exclamation now and then and the
sound of the Victrola. Toby sleeps by my chair. Nance, in
blue, has gone out just now to walk with Mother. Peg is on
the sofa with *Don Quixote*. — She was reading an OZ book
before, but I got her to try this by showing her the pictures
and telling her, — "Berta loved it when she was younger
than you even."

We skated this morning on the reservoir, — Zippy, Mlle.

Father to Daughter

and I. It was pretty there. One bank is the side of a steep hill, you know, with rocks, birches and ever-greens on it and under that was new ice, and black. Toby ran after me everywhere, the way he does. Mr. Eaton came, and the Ashwell's with two children, and Mr. Brewer with one. Pretty Mrs. Harden sat on the bank and wrapped herself in our blue blanket, which became her. Zippy tied her scarf to Toby's collar and he, following me, pulled her around. — But I saw a man coming on foot across the ice and I knew what was up. I took Toby ashore and asked Zip to keep him and skated toward the man. "Whose dog is that?" said he. "Mine," I said. "Well, you must keep him off the ice." "Alright," I said and I tied him to a fence post. When we got our skates off which took long, for we had to stop now and then to warm our fingers, I went to Mrs. Harden to ask her to keep our blanket for us and Mrs. Warren was there and asked us to come to tea this afternoon, and I thought 'Confound it,' and said, "We'd love to," — which was half true, for Mother would. (I see Nance coming home, her coat sticking out stiffly, using a stick for a cane; — and Mother clutching the front of her buttonless coat.) Zippy has written you a letter and marked it PRIVATE and has left it here on the desk. Now I'll play deck tennis with Mlle. and I'll write you more tonight. I'll write my loved one every night the last thing and dream about her; — and may the letter find her happy and well.

Sunday Night

Do you think this plan of writing in bed will work? Old Dr. Johnson did it, and Swift wrote most of the *Journal to Stella* that way, by candlelight too. — But not with a fountain pen. Still it goes pretty well. We went to the Warrens after a call from Mr. and Mrs. Adams. It turned out to be about confirmation. Mother promised to deliver over Zippy and Peg, which seemed to me reckless. She has not yet consulted them, and Zippy holds strong views on how she shall spend her time, even if not on theology. My pen has run out but I have a pencil.

Mrs. Warren met us at the door. We were between two rooms, — one crowded, the other almost empty. Mother chose one, I the other. You know which took which. I talked to Mrs. Self, — rather she talked to me about her pictures and stories. She was in riding trousers. Then Mrs. Harden came in and sat on the sofa between us and I talked to her. Mother told me afterward that she saw Mrs. Strite who said you were the loveliest girl she had ever seen. — Its getting late. Good night dear girl. I wish I were to see you at breakfast.

January 23rd

We've gone back to spring, but the stars are shining. I took off Zip's comfortable before I got to bed. My clock struck this morning and, there being no Bert here to call me, I missed my train; and I reached the platform for the one you take just behind a pair of very high heeled shoes which supported Juliette. It was one of those talky days, — no time for work. S.S. Van Dine must have talked for an hour or more. When he became ill three years ago it must have seemed his ruin. It was really his good fortune. Two years in bed reading mystery stories made him their master and that is bringing him a fortune fast. I gave Zip for her birthday a book of pictures by Caldecort who drew for the *London Graphic* in the 70s and 80s, — humorous pictures of English Country life, mostly of hunting and shooting. They are as good as Du Maurier's though not so funny. Peg and Zip love them, and you will too. Peg, I can see, isn't going to get very far with *Don Quixote*. I must remember to get from Mother the names of those school books, and order them sent to Aunt Molly. I hit Mlle. on her side with a ring at deck tennis. She said later it pained her very much and I couldn't tell if she was joking or not. So I took up the telephone, keeping my thumb on the hook, asked for 88, and pretended to tell Dr. O'Shaunnessy Mlle. Demarest was badly hurt and he must come right over. That caused a Gaelic commotion and brought out the truth. — Oh, its 11:30 and I must sleep, — as I hope you're doing now, and well dear girl.

January 24th

Tomorrow I'll mail this to my Berta. Peggy came to dinner in that blue skirt, and the brown blouse that has the blue points on the collar: — the dress my Bertha wore ever so long ago at 112 Rockview when she was a brave little girl who rode on her Daddys shoulders in the Watchung Mountains. I was kept late in the office for letters to sign. Mother and Peg met me at Darien. Peg ran toward me under the platform light and her cheeks were almost as red as her leather jacket. We all sat in the front seat and Mother told me how well Janey did in the afternoon in dancing school. The road was shiney with rain — spring rain. Its been warm since Sunday. What a winter! At this rate, it will be like midsummer when you come back.

"Copey" resigned last week and there was quite a lot in the papers about him. I got home Saturday very tired, and was lying down, though the day was fine, when Miss Wyckoff called up to read me a telegram from the Harvard Crimson asking for a hundred word telegram of appreciation. I said, "Oh, I guess I'll forget it." — But then my conscience got to work and kept bothering me. I wrote out a telegram and walked down to Cody's and sent it; — and I'm glad I did because my telegram and one other were all that were printed, — and the other was even worse than mine. I imagine the requests arrived at such an awkward time, Saturday P.M., that some were not received and others were neglected. — But Conrad Aiken wrote a good piece. He said Copey's resignation could be only *technical.* — You might as well talk of wrapping up a flood and putting it away in a drawer. I know Copey'll give me the deuce for my telegram. He'll say — "You are my publisher. Why didn't you mention the Reader." He's discovered that I'm Secy. of Scribner's now and always refers to me as such, — and so does the Crimson.

I'm writing at Mother's desk. The rain is dripping into the puddle outside the window and I can see it shining, from the street light, in the hollows of the lawn. Oh, Berta, if I get you safely home do you think you'll ever get away again? Not till you're of age and can legally defy me.

Your ever loving
Daddy

Maxwell Perkins

January 26th

Zippy is furiously writing at her story. She is sitting on the arm of the big brown chair at the blue covered table, dressed in her red suit. Janey is in that reddish, tight, french suit in which she looks so well, sitting by Mother on the sofa at the side of the living room. Its a cold night. — I can feel the cold from the window by this desk. We shall have skating, I think. We have had no snow here but snow covered the country below Talmadge Hill today, though thinly; — yet N.Y. had none.

I had a gay letter from Hemingway today, from Switzerland. He said he had not written for some weeks because for two he had been blind, — though now he could see. He had been skiing in Switzerland. Doing that, you wear goggles, for the snow glare. Once he fell very hard and the glass of both lenses was broken to bits, but hurt him not the least. That night he went to say goodnight to his little boy in the dark. The boy put his arm up and the nail of his finger cut across his father's eyeball. He says he thought for a time he would never see again.

Uncle Allie called me up today to say that Aunt Molly wrote that Aunt Mary was doing wonderfully well; — was not nearly so uncomfortable as they expected, took a great interest in all that went on in the hospital and was learning everything about it. Aunt Molly said she almost thought "she rather enjoyed the experience."

Mr. Scribner goes away tomorrow for two months. I had lunch with him and his son, and we had a pleasant time too. Generally before he goes away he is worried and worries us. Today he let it go with saying that he'd bet an English publisher he doesn't like with whom I am negotiating a contract would "get the best of me before he was through if I regarded him as a Gentleman"; and that "things were in good shape but that we'd all be in trouble before his train was out from under the river." — These things he says with humor, you know Bert. I've liked him increasingly ever since I've known him, — some years now too.

January 27th

Dearest darling, this is the night of Mr. Beaux Arts Ball; that's why I'm here. I've just come back from a very, very champagney dinner at Mr. Scribner's, among the nominally best people. Really Berta — Society may be something somewhere, but its not much here; and betwixt you and me I doubt if it ever was anything to speak of, anywhere, as such. Where Swift was there was society, — or Johnson, or perhaps Addison, or Byron or any man of genius. Or indeed, Mr. Scott Fitzgerald, or Padraic Colum (who is now in town). And there were ladies, and one was Mary Wortley Montagu, and I've ordered for my darling Bert this day a book called, "A Portrait of Lady Montagu" which should be here by the end of March, with luck; — for it was well reviewed in the *Spectator* and all the people in whom you are interested are in it, — those of the 18th Century. Well, there was not, at this dinner, one word of intelligence spoken, — though all was good humor, what with the champagne. Why not? There was a Master of Hounds in his pink coat, — a dumb-bell; two men in supposedly African costumes, one Charley Scribner; one with the red trousers and blue coat of the French Foreign Legion — an oldish "gentleman" who drank too much; and ladies dressed in baggy trousers. Mother looked well in a hoop-skirt of white, and I made Charley promise he'd get her safely home to Bopa's.

I'm staying here because I could not sleep a wink if I were in the house where Mother was to come, — sometime; — and Charley promised he would see her safely home. I'm desolated with you on the sea and Mother at this crazy ball and the others away off in New Canaan; — But, I hope to sleep and now will try. — About you I don't dare much to think.

Your loving daddy
Maxwell E. Perkins

January 28th

Dearest darling: — The Ball is over and we're all home. — so *that's* off our minds, and I guess forever since Mother didn't much enjoy it. Your pictures have come and they are good. — I shall have one enlarged so far as can be done, and framed, for it is a picture of a truly high, noble, character, and later generations will be proud of it; — and girls will wish to be like *that* girl, and will be the better for it. The Colums have come. Mrs. C. came to my office today looking rosy and plump and bearing an Alpine stock — a cane with a metal point, and a mountain goat's horn for handle. — This was a present for me.

Do you know the look of dry, wind-driven snow in the corners of window panes at night. — That I see when I turn my head to the left. Its a true winter's night. The ground is thinly whited, — but the road is mostly bared by the wind, — only streaked and spotted white. — So we got no more skating after all, — though Zip was invited to a skating party for this evening. She didn't want to go and asked me for an excuse. I said, hold a piece of ice in your hand while you telephone and say you have a little cold. — She said later she had done this but had forgot to get the ice.

I've been lying about all afternoon, — being tired from the dinner, which was, for me, late. I found a magnificent short story by Ambrose Bierce about the Civil War. First I read it myself, then to Zippy, then to Pegs, and this evening, to Mother. I wish, I wish, — I must stop thinking of it — that I might read it once more, to my darling Berta.

January 29th

I read that story again today; — to Miss Bailey. She brought me a real compliment: A publisher proposed a contract to her which involved a point of ethics, that is honour, at least in this case; and he said, "if there's any question about it in your mind ask Maxwell Perkins, for I'll accept him as final upon a point of ethics." That pleased me, from a publisher.

We've had a clear, cold day of the sort that comes after a

clean, dry snowstorm. The children had their sleds out, and Nancy took a walk. — But now she has a cold. Last night, just as I stopped writing you she began to cry, as Peggy who was sleeping in your room called down to tell us. She was very cold. Mother wrapped her in a blanket and brought her down before the fire, and I held her while Mother warmed some milk and got out the hot water bottle, — and this morning she seemed well, but later she began to sneeze. I wish we'd kept her in bed all day. — But its not a bad cold, and though at one time she was so cross that when Mlle. spoke of the snow as *white*, Nance asserted, "it's black," and even when confronted with the overwhelming evidence of the landscape would concede no more than that "it's partly white and partly black," she has been mostly happy all the day. — Much decenter to me than usual in fact.

Do you know when I was glad we had no radio? Two nights after you sailed. They told me at Bopa's that on that windy evening the entertainment was suddenly broken off for an S.O.S. call. — A ship was in danger. Bopa was frightened. After some time they learned it was a freighter, — but what a terrible interval that would have been in *this* family!

You should have heard the account Mother gave Miss Bailey of the Ball, — the veritable echo of the hard things I had said about it in advance; — but, come next year, distance will have lent enchantment: — She'll be eager again to go.

Well, dear Bert, if letters like most to be warmly received when they come, a letter that you write me will be blessed among letters.

Your loving daddy,
Maxwell E. Perkins

Last night I had bad dreams, — of storms at sea. But today Raymond Whitcomb said the *Carinthia* arrived on time at Madeira; — and the Mediterranean should be calm, whatever it was in the days of the wily Ulysses.

Our snow is now soggy and mists obscure the moon, — at least they did as tonight we hummed along the road from Darien, for I had missed my train. I lunched with Charley Scribner at the Union Club, and first we had a cocktail at the bar, and so we did not get back till two thirty, which made me late. Helen Wills' Ms. came in and seemed to be excellently done; and our Ms. on boxing by an ex-prize fighter and one Dr Billik who gave me the sweater I wear at deck tennis. Our Athletic Library, which I have slowly developed from the time you were not more than two, will be much stronger for these. — It contains now some dozen volumes, and every one sells steadily each season. Now, tomorrow I must get at a library of Detective novels, which will be successful, but, for some weeks, troublesome.

Mrs. Colum came here for lunch and Mother motored her around in search of a house, and they found one on East Avenue, near the crest of the hill. — They'll be in it before your ship gets home. It's after ten and I must go to bed.

Your loving Daddy

January 31st

Darling: We need you badly here. We're driven mad over the area of rectangular boxes, which only you could find, — that is, the area. I have found boxes, to the number of several; — but each one Zippy measured by a ruler with despair: the dimensions involved fractions of the inch. If only one came out to the even inch, she says, or you were here to help, all would be well.

I'll get this off tomorrow that it may surely catch the prescribed ship, though another day is allowed. Nance is quite well again, after a days orange juice fast, and very jolly, — as much opposed to me as ever.

I passed a bad day with much work to do and no chance to do it because of callers. A day of chatter. And tomorrow I must go to a publishers luncheon, and the day after to Alice Duer Miller's for lunch; — and that, because, not wanting to go, I knew I could not make an excuse sound convincing. — She is writing a novel for which I gave her the plot. — So is John Biggs, and that one will, I think, be very fine.

Peg has read over 400 pages of *Don Quixote* and now likes it much. — That and *Pickwick* in one winter is something to have done, — more profitable in the end than many school lessons. Peg told me that she saw Lida today and that both she and her sister, Lainey, had written you letters. Peg took readily to the idea of confirmation, and Zippy reluctantly. Peg did ask how she was to know whether this church was the best one to join. Mother said, "That is just why you are to go to Mr. Adams. He will explain it all to you." And she was angry with me when I said, "And of course there's no doubt that his explanation will be impartial." But I thought Peg's question was to the point.

Goodnight my dearest darling. May this letter find you happy and well, in the land of Egypt.

Your loving daddy,
Maxwell E. Perkins

February 3, 1928

Dearest Berta: — We're in the miserablest, grey, damp, weather. — Have been since Sunday. Mother has a sore throat, Mlle. has such a sore throat she can't eat, I have a sore throat, but only on one side: — and Peggy and Zippy, upon reflection, think that they have sore throats. Everybody seems to have something. Janey is in bed, upset, and has been for two days. — And the Hedgehog saw his shadow on Candlemas Day, so we're in for six weeks more of sore throats, and miserable, damp, grey weather. — But the sun is shining somewhere and I hope the place is the Mediterranean. I hear Mother sneezing now!

The children's reports came today. Jane's was all one could ask. Peggy's and Zippy's were better than on any previous rendering, — though both were in attention, "spasmodic." Peggy "defaces her books"; — and so between ourselves does Zippy, though Miss Dudley hasn't discovered it yet. Peg has read the whole first part of *Don Quixote*, and I thought that enough; — the second is less good.

I went yesterday to lunch in an apartment on the very edge of the East River, just below the Queensboro Bridge where we walked that night; — opposite Blackwell's stand, with its grim prison. The balcony outside the window actually overhangs the water. Boats go up an down all the time, and you hear their whistles. You could sit there all day and watch the boats in the swift river, and their white plumes of steam, or grey plumes of smoke; and the big rocks at the end of the island that cut through the current. At night, in bed you could hear the whistles, — the hoarse fog horns on foggy nights. We used to hear them at Newport in the harbour.

I mailed you today, a letter from Zippy and one from Mother, and an envelope containing the proofs of your pictures. I sent the boy out to put them in a mail box so they would surely get off in time. You've been away two weeks tonight. — Thats a quarter of your trip, to take the cheerfulest view of the thing.

I just went up to say goodnight to Jen. She's all curled up

in your bed with her little blue wrapper on top of the covers.
I told her I was writing you how excellent was her report.

February 4th

Today we had a sudden burst of spring. Rivulets ran down
the gutters and films of water lay over the ice on the ponds,
and the sun was bright and warm. Peggy, who went in with
her class to see the *Merchant of Venice* came in at 7:30,
flushed and complaining of the heat; — but she com-
plained more, and with indignation at the treatment of
Shylock, "that poor jew!"

I came out late myself, for Capt. Thomason, who wrote
Fix Bayonets etc. turned up. We had lunch together. He is a
fine fellow. What is better to talk about than war? He likes
the books I like, and the men. I told him he must come up
to Windsor and talk to Uncle Tommy, of whom he knows.
He has tried to get me to go with him over the field of
Gettysburg and has done it several times himself. He says he
cannot see how Lee ever thought he could break Meade's
Centre, considering the strength of the Yankee position on
Cemetary Ridge. Yet Pickett's men, unsupported, did get to
the top of it.

I brought the children a volume of Charles Keene's pictures and jokes from *Punch*; — better, in fact, than Du
Maurier's. Zip and Peg are delighted with it. Mlle.'s throat is
very sore. — She has stayed in bed all this day and Mother
took care of Nance. Jen is again up and about. — She ought
to be in bed now for it is twenty minutes of nine. Mother
and I and Nance took a drive in the car, — it was too wet for
a walk. — The country is covered with soggy snow. We drove
to Silvermine and crossed the river at the house the Pagits
used to have, — slowly so that Nance could see the falls. We
stopped at the French farmhouse, decided it would be un-

comfortable and hard to heat, and came back slowly. The air was soft, but everything looked untidy and dismal, as always in a thaw.

February 5th

Peg, in a blue sailor blouse, is sitting in the chair between the french windows, looking at the Keene pictures. Zippy is restlessly searching for a "*modern* book." She read Scott Fitzgerald's *Tales of the Jazz Age* and begs for more Fitzgerald. Nemesis!! What?

Jane had a swelling under her eye. It turned out to be an abcess; — and this afternoon the Dr. came and looked at it, and said it should be cut open. — So we took Jane up to the bathroom and she sat there and watched the Dr. get out all sorts of knives and scissors and bandages. She sat and watched. Then he took a knife with a hooked point and cut right into her. —And she never turned a hair. She is just as you were about those things and I admire her.

We went to a tea at the Watts, — a farewell tea to the Strites who are sailing for North Africa. First every one took a horrible present to the Strites "from the attic." Mother took a shield you children used in one of the plays. Others took horrible clocks, and bathing girls made of metal, and metal sailor boys. The house was full of these things, and what they will do with them I don't know. I daresay they'll be the happier to go away. At the Watts there was a great roar of conversation, tobacco smoke, and some rather good punch. I tried to find out from the Strite girl, at Smith, about girls' colleges. She is a nice, German looking girl, — broad, flaxen haired, and ruddy. — All these people are nice people, — a finer aggregation of decent men and women I never saw in any town; — but I'm against all aggregations. I was trying to explain why to Mother by this illustration:

Sometimes, when introduced to a person, you make out to shake hands, and somehow miss, and your hands slide over each other, and fumble. They fail to grip. — And so do minds at teas and such gatherings. Language is a poor means of communication at best. Several times when I've been very troubled I've walked up and down with you — even when you were only twelve years old or so — and you've seemed to know I *was* troubled and have done me more good than anyone could have done with words. What are words? Air! What is air? Nothing.

February Sixth:

Darling Bert — I would never have let you go on this trip if I had realized weeks would pass before I heard a word about you. Heaven knows how long we shall still have to wait.

It's very cold again, and clear. There must be skating. The moon is full, — very large and yellow like an October moon. It was almost too cold for deck tennis but we managed to play our three sets, as usual. This night I began to read *Henry Esmond*, sitting on the new sofa between Peggy and Zip, both of whom drew pictures while they listened. Janey looks quite well now, even as to her eye.

Mother went this afternoon to a tea at the Katzenbach's where Miss Whitridge is, with two black eyes. She was motoring up through Virginia. There was snow on the ground, and under it, though she did not know, ice. She was running fast around a curve. The car skidded in a circle. That is all she knows. She came to in a farm house. The car had run into a telegraph pole. People in another car had come along and found her unconscious. The engine was broken. — Suppose she had been away out in the country, and no one had come? The car would not go. I won't write any more tonight. This letter will be so long by the date when it should be mailed that I doubt you'll read it through anyhow.

February 8th,

We're in a fog. — Such a one that while playing deck tennis it streamed about in the piazza like smoke from a cigarette; — and all yesterday it dripped, dripped, dripped, and, says the papers, so will do tomorrow. We must stay in that night, — to dine at the Laroque's. And now Copey is sending me wires to come up and see him on a *Saturday*, of all days. I'll end by going too.

Yesterday came to "Miss Peggy Perkins," four letters from the Philippine Islands. — Answers to some letters she wrote last summer on the behest of Miss Uhlen. — Letters from natives there, one half Chinese, who said she was a "fat girl" and gave her dimensions which were appalling, each one signed "Your little pal," or "Your unknown pal," each imploring an answer — "Hurry!"

Another piece of news is this: Lainey told Zippy that Mrs. Ellsworth said she considered Nance "neither pretty nor attractive." Zippy said she would have liked to have slapped Lainey. She told her that she felt sure that Nance was very pretty. Lainey apparently did not commit herself to an opinion.

Each night now, while Janey's undressing we read *Henry Esmond*, — Zippy, Peg, and I; and they both love it. Oh Berta darling, are we never to have a letter from you?

February 10th

This night came Bliss Carmen while we were still at dinner, in his belled trousers and sombrero and with his blackthorn stick. Mother said to Janey; "Say goodnight to Mr. Carmen;

and when you're grown up you'll tell how a great poet came to see your Mother and Father," — which Bliss accepted with a blink. Soon thereafter came the Colums, and greatly admired my velvet coat.

Last night we dined at the Laroque's. They too are on the river. How the sharp lights shone from the buildings on the island opposite, and along its edge, in a row. The river looked black and hard. The tugs went up and down with their soft, red and green lights glowing.

There were many people and we sat around a circular table. Mother sat next a fat, bald man who said "I went to St. Paul's School with your husband." "Oh no!" said Mother. "His father went there. It must have been with him." Poor Lorillard Spencer. I remember so well when Mr. Jenkins, Latin teacher — he worshipped Caesar and we would get him talking of Caesar till he forgot to make us recite — took him across his knee in class and spanked him. I took in a prettyish blonde named Mrs. Gray. Her old husband, next Mrs. Laroque, called out that my father was his father's partner; he was the son of John Gray, Judge Gray, for whom I was almost named. Mrs. Arthur Train sat on my other hand, so I had a goodish time. — But it was a very Victorian affair, heavy and slow. Most people settled down afterward to somnolence or bridge. I sat in the window with Mrs. Laroque and watched the lights shining on the bright, black river, till Mrs. Train, God bless her, offered to drive us home.

We got Grandma's cable yesterday and felt better for it. I hope it told the truth. You left us three weeks ago tonight. When shall we get a letter?

I came down at 8.30 this A.M. in Bopa's house to find Bopa in a dressing gown solemnly following the parrot from the drawing room into the dining room, — both walking with magnificent and stately deliberation as if engaged in some affair of high import. I felt insignificant and ridiculous before such gravity. — Anyway, I always feel the disapproval of that parrot.

February 12th

I didn't write last night because Mrs. Colum and Miss Bailey came, and stayed late, and I was tired. This day was a fine one, yet we did little; — slept till 9.30 and then read newspapers. Zippy played her banjo, sitting by the fire. She can now trill somewhat. We had turkey for dinner, but Nance, who was cross from her nap, would have none of it, nor of anything else, — certainly not of me. Zippy and I motored through Ridgefield with the idea of going to the Port of Missing Men. But the road to it was so deeply rutted that it could not be done, — a pity for the day was fine and that great spread of country would have been beautiful in the sunshine. There was a brightness over everything that suggested spring. Zippy and I talked about you and praised you, and agreed that you had an inferiority complex but were getting over it now, and said how odd it was that such a person could have one.

The Colums came to supper, — Padraic very neatly dressed — the first time I ever saw him so — in blue. I spoke of the ballad Zip and Lainey had written and we got Zip to bring it, he read much of it aloud, making ludicrous comments, so that everyone was laughing, — most of all Zippy.

February 13th

This day, which was very fine, and a holiday, I bought, at Silliman's, a bicycle. I walked downtown and on Main Street near Runyon's, saw Toby. — So I investigated Runyon's: there, in a booth, ordering ice cream, were all my children but you. They had permission from Mother.

I rode from Silliman's out South Main St. to the road that leads to the Cemetary, down which I coasted; and then up through the woods, sometimes walking by necessity, to the top. Then I rode about in that upland region, sometimes on trails and finally came to that hill where we have often gone and talked of building; — the one from which you see the two white steeples near our house. They were clear and bright today. I coasted all the way from the hill through the woods, — almost falling several times on account of the deep ruts — and rode around the Cemetary pond, and then home.

The Colums came here for tea; — Mother had been with them in their new house where workmen are painting etc. and she brought them back. I was reading a Ms. and I have another to begin and so can write no more.

Janey, in her pink knitted dress, is reading in the big chair at the end of the living room. Zippy and Peggy are wrestling noisily in the big brown armchair in the study, and Mother, with her legs tucked up, is reading in the other big chair by the black round table.

We all long for a letter from you, darling.

Your loving daddy,
Maxwell E. Perkins

Friday, February 17

Darling Berta: —
We got, several days ago, your two letters from Gibralta, and Grandma's one. Mine was in the office. I thought it was from some English author. Then Mother came to the office with Nance (for a night at Bopa's) with the other and Grandma's. I went home with all three. Jen was in bed with a

Father to Daughter

cough (it sounds like whooping cough) and I sat on Zip's bed with Zip and Peg, and read all three letters aloud. Everyone was delighted with them. Zip was envious of your 'luck.' — That was the night before last, I now remember. Mrs. Colum came after dinner, and she and I talked till eleven, so I could not write, and last night came a meeting of School Trustees at the Ashwell's, and lasted late; and I was very tired after it. We hope for more letters soon. Jen is reading *Castle Blair* with concentration. — But we must now go to bed and I must stop for a bit to read *Henry Esmond.* — What a beautiful book that is. I was astonished to find it so good, — a finer thing than *Vanity Fair.*

Miss Bailey came in. She has just gone, — I drove her home through sleet that rain has just become — and it is eleven o'clock. So I can't write more. I read her another story by Ambrose Bierce, a remarkable writer people hardly know of. He professed to hate war and then at the age of seventy walked off into Mexico in order to see war once more, — and was shot, by Villa's men, or so they think. I'll go on tomorrow night, darling.

February 18th

That sleet turned to snow and fell all night long, and all this day, — a still, heavy snow. Everything is now thickly covered. Each twig even of the bushes behind the stone wall across Seminary St. is four times its size with snow. It is the first true Winter's night we've had, — for it's cold too. — But by the look of the light now'a days, I think spring can *not* be far behind.

I tell you Bert, I think Jen has whooping cough. We'll have to make the best of it and see her through. I wouldn't mind Nance having it so much. What was the name of that medicine — Roach's Ambrocation! I hope I'll remember it.

Zip says, "Bert and Jane have all the luck in *this* family. Of course we have whooping cough in the summer; and Jane gets a vacation out of it!" Zip is now at her banjo, practising. She's trilling, and mighty well. She and Peg are great companions. While I read to them tonight they both drew on opposite pages of the same notebook.

Your Mother takes riding lessons. She's bought herself a wonderful, complete, equipment including boots. She goes to that place near Darien and the man who teaches her is the one named Jack who used to teach you, — the one who had the Brookses Stable.

February 19th

The Dr. was just here to innoculate Janey and Nance for the whoops — Nance said "Oh!" when the needle went in, and then smiled — and he took a look at Linda who had stayed in bed with a headache: — She's got the mumps! Isn't that a nice situation. Got it at the movies! You'd think she was old enough to keep away from movies, wouldn't you? Mother hasn't heard this pleasant news yet, for she has been out, probably at the Colum's all afternoon. It is now six o'clock. I think I hear her.

Zippy and I had a game of deck tennis, at which she is very good. — But she says you are better. The other children played in the snow. They made a good slide down the hill and Jane used it a good part of the day, which was a fine one. I spent most of it on a Ms. not yet finished, — except for two games of deck tennis and a snowy walk with Zip up past the Homewood, which Toby enjoyed. He romped with two Airedales in the snow.

Father to Daughter

February 21st

Yes, Jen undoubtedly has the whoops. Wish us luck! The children had a holiday on Lincoln's Birthday in the idea that they would go to school on Washington's. But now they're to have that day off too, so many children are away, — with mumps. May we all be mumpless when you return. Mlle. told me Jen would not mind her about putting on proper clothes to go out. — And now it's so important she should! I took her to the back of the living room and talked to her. She began to argue but I told her I would not argue with her because I knew she would beat me at that. At last I said: "When Berta was little I would talk over a matter like this and explain its importance, and she would overcome her spirit and understand about it and would promise to do right. — And then I felt perfectly safe, for she *always* remembered and *always* kept her word." And then Jane promised me. Berta, lots of people, and good ones, have lived a life-time and done less good than you have done already by the influence of your character on the other children, — to say nothing of your daddy. (I must stop now and read to Peg and Zip.)

After the reading I went into my room to dress for deck tennis. I heard Nance crying and ran to her. She was shivering all over. It was very cold in the room. She stopped crying when I said I would call Mother, — which I did. Within two minutes not only was Mother there, but Zip, and Peg, and Jane, in her wrapper. We turned on the electric heater and soon had Nance warmed up, but she hated to take some medicine Mother brought her. She fought against it. Mother said: "Don't you love Mother?" "No" said Nance "I love Daddy." — And truly she does come nearer to doing so than when you left us. When I came home tonight she offered to go upstairs with me and watch me wash, — and did so. One morning when I was dressing she passed through the hall with Mlle. and stopped to tap on the bathroom door, and when I opened it, she stayed and talked to me. That night I asked her if she wouldn't do that again the next morning. She said: "I might."

February 22nd

Mother is reading her story to Mr. and Mrs. Colum, who dined here with the family. Jane and Peg have gone to bed and Zippy is reading. I spent most of the day, but for deck tennis, reading Ms., — though we went with Miss Bailey to the Colum's for tea, in their new house. Mother showed them, and they admired, your pictures. This morning was bright, and all the children were out in the snow, which is thinning, showing patches of dead grass; but a damp haze came down in the afternoon. All was dreary. I think rain is coming on. (The story is done and the Colum's think it a splendid one.) They have gone now, afoot, Padraic taking a walking stick he left here some days ago.

I'll mail this letter tomorrow, to be sure it gets the right ship. If only you mailed us one at Athens we should hear from you soon. Do you read every night in *The Spirit of Man?*
Your loving daddy,
Maxwell E. Perkins

There now seems to be some doubt if Linda has the mumps: — not in her own mind, nor ever was. She always denied it. Her swelling has gone, and her temperature. But she has other swellings on her face and it may be mild erisipilis, — how ever you spell it. — But Jen surely has whooping cough and the Dr. today innoculated her and Nance. This time Nance cried and said "It hurts"; she saw the needle go in.

Write all you can.
Daddy

Father to Daughter

February 25, 1928

Darling Berta: —

Poor Janey has begun to whoop a little now, but her coughing spells are quite far apart. We hope she may have a light
case. By the time you get home she should be almost well.

We keep jumping from spring to winter. — And now it's
winter. I think snow is coming, for though you can see stars,
the young moon is blurred by a haze. Zip and I took a bicycle ride this afternoon, and though I had on a knitted cap
I was so cold that, to protect my ears, I took off my woolen
gloves and put them over them inside it. We rode a long way
on frozen roads so deeply rutted that we had often to walk
even on level ground. We came home past the Pinkhams,
and there with the children was a Great Mastiff. We were far
up the hill beyond, Zippy a hundred feet behind me, when
this Mastiff came baying after us. He came at a trot. I walked
slowly so Zip would gradually catch up, and told her just to
walk quietly. He come very close to her before she reached
me. When she did we walked side by side between our bicycles. He followed sulkily for a long way. I hate such dogs,
who, if they are cross, can do such damage.

Later, going up another hill, we saw coming down another enormous dog, — a Newfoundland. We knew he
would be friendly. As Zippy said, he was like Toby, but ten
times as big. He was followed by Mr. and Mrs. Stokes to
whom he belonged. They said he was only a puppy, eight
months old. He reminded me of Emperor, a Newfoundland
who lived with us when we were children.

We were mighty glad to reach home at last. — We got
Mlle. to make us chocolate, and drank it before the fire.

February 26th

Jane has been roached and ambrocated and put to bed, and I've just finished reading *Henry Esmond* to the children. Zippy is sitting in the very middle of the new sofa, under the light, playing her banjo. Mother, in black velvet, is on the other sofa; and Peg is reading by the fire. — We need a fire too, for it is cold, though fair.

Mother and I went to the Colum's at tea time. Mrs. Colum is sick abed and while Mother was seeing her I talked to Padraic, and somehow we got to discussing Xenophon, and thought what a wonderful biography his would be. For he was a wonder! — A cavalry officer and philosopher and naturalist, friend of all the great Athenians including Socrates at whose noble death he was. His life was active and adventurous, and yet reflective; — and he wrote about all of it. — But only a scholar in Greek could adequately write it. You'll read his *Anabasis*, about the coming down from Persia in desperate retreat, of the Ten Thousand Greeks whom he led; — and for all that he was studying along the dangerous way to the Sea, the plants, the animals, and the peoples.

Zip and I went for a bicycle ride this morning, but some dampness in the cold air made it bite to the bone. We only rode out the Silvermine road — a few people were skating on the mill pond — and then passed the Self's where the dogs all barked at us, and back by the other road. That ride and a little deck tennis was all the exercise I had.

Linda did not have mumps; — and whatever she had she's recovered from. She leaves us for Windsor tomorrow and a new cook is coming from Stamford. I hope she'll stay with us.

February 27th

Bert, the whooping cough is a terrible thing to see, as I've always thought. Poor Janey looks so tired. She's been going now for nearly three weeks and ought soon to reach the worst stage, — which lasts for three weeks. How distinctly the smell of Roach's Ambrocation brings back that awful summer when we were all of us sick and coughing.

We got your letter from Athens today. Mother and Zip met me at Darien. It was dark, but Zip read the letter aloud to Mother as we drove, while I held above it her flickering cigarette lighter. — Only I wish you wrote letters ten times as long. I'm afraid one of mine to you will never reach you; it was marked to go by the *Ile de France* which, for some outrageous reason, never sailed. — Every one is indignant with the Post Office about it.

I'm to lunch tomorrow with a Dr Billik who has written an excellent book on boxing; — we're to discuss one on "Keeping fit". The secret of it is, "Don't work"; as a young man with a cold and a whiskey flask told me when I, with a cold met him at the Harvard Club bar.

February 28th

I think the little Norman farmhouse is one of the prettiest houses in the world. Two lights shine outside it every night, reddish lights that hang from the walls, the white walls. Surely a nice man must have planned such a house.

Poor Janey — She coughed less today, but she stayed in bed. It's a horrible disease. No rest, no food. She's been at it now little short of three weeks, — but that leaves worse to come and six weeks to go. Well, we lived through it once and must do it again. And must we then see Nancy suffer?

At the gate of the Darien train, I met a beautiful black and white Setter, and Mrs. Self. She'd just received him from England as a gift from her father; — also an English saddle which a porter was bearing. She was stopped by the

Guard for lack of a muzzle, but that we got at the baggage checking room and I led the dog up forward and left him in the baggage car. We sat together in the train, she reading a book I had in my bag, and I another. — English books about famous crimes which I hope we may publish. She doesn't look well, nor seem happy, and she's such a nice, fine person. Why can't they let her be happy, — those who keep the planets spinning and reel off the troubles, I mean.

Mr. Adams is run down and so will run away for six months, — out your way, the Mediterranean. He promises in the fall to summon the Bishop especially for the sake of Zip and Peg. They seem willing enough to wait, though Peg anyhow was seriously interested.

I'll mail this tomorrow darling and may it find you well and happy at Nice.

Your loving daddy
Maxwell E. Perkins

March 4, 1928

Darling Berta: — I've written you to the last point nominated on the cruise folder — Nice — but I'll try so to address this letter that you will get it before you sail from Southampton, or on the day you do sail.

Janey seems much better. We have some new medicine that appears to be remarkably effective. Today she has had no actual paroxysms, nor yesterday. The truth is, she never has coughed as alarmingly as did Zip and Peg, — and you though you kept it secret. Her trouble has come from her frailty and from being made so often sick. But now, if she stays in bed, that may be avoided.

This has been a beautiful day, though cold. Mother and Zip went to church. Peg and I rode off on bicycles, — out

Father to Daughter

the Silvermine road, down to the river, filmed with black ice, and along that rutted road to the reservoir. — *That* was mostly bare of ice, and the waters, roughed by wind, sparkled blue. We sat on a rock there and looked at the yellow hills at the end of the lake, and prophesied that spring would come, — indeed was on the very edge of coming now. We took Toby. Since I got my bicycle, we have had no walks. He has sat or lain at my chair-side eyeing me as if I had wronged him. So I took him for all the risk from motors. But we met with few. His only danger came from me. He ran once right before my wheel and it went right over him. It did no harm. He shook himself, and then frisked about, and jumped on me in apology.

We motored last night to the Riter's for dinner. Mrs. Riter was away and no lady was there but Mother. There was a third man, a broker I inferred. It seemed to me a very dull evening, but Mother enjoyed it; — And I enjoyed the sleep that followed it when we got home at mid-night.

March 7th

On the fifth, I developed such a headache in the afternoon that I went to bed the moment I got home. I slept for twelve hours; — I think the headache came from weariness. — Overexercise on Sunday. Then, last night came Mrs. Colum, a late-stayer. No time was left to write when she went.

Janey gets on, but her eyes are all swollen from coughing so that her eyebrows point upward Chinese-like. — She is improving though, and Nance, who has coughed now for some three weeks, develops very slowly. She is no trouble to speak of. And soon we should have spring days. I've had a letter from Aunt Molly that says all the children have been sick with sore throats and she too, and in bed. — But that is over now. And she told us that Louie had scarlet fever. So

Mother called up Uncle Edward and found she was all but over it and that the other children, who were sent elsewhere, had passed the time of danger.

Your letter to Zippy from Cairo came this morning and delighted her. I read it to Janey when I got home. I'll copy for you a poem Zip wrote for her English: —

ODE TO A BOX OF CHOCOLATES

O strong, or heavy box of pale sea green,
And tied together with a shimmering bow,
O what sweet mystery beneath thy lid,
Lies there in calm repose, I long to know.

And when thou art opened, Ah! what toothsome sight!
Each lying in its fluted paper cup,
Plump and serene, attractive to the eye
And waiting calmly to be eaten up.

There is another poem, "Dancing School," but not as good a one.

We've been having fine weather now for some three weeks, though cold. — But its a poor month in which to have it because there's so little you can do. The ice is too rough now for skating.

March 8th

Mother has gone to the movies — *The Student Prince,* and poor Zip was mad to go, but had used up her turns early in the month, and I wouldn't allow it. I all but did yield though, — if she'd pressed me a bit further — But I'm glad I did not. She, of all of you, needs to learn restraint. Janey is much better, and Nance, it really seems, is to have a light

Father to Daughter

case. She coughs, but only as one does with a cold.

I had a useless kind of day, or rather afternoon. Mr. Burt wired me an invitation to lunch and Jesse Lynch Williams heard he was coming up and got him on the wire and persuaded him, with me, to go for a cocktail to his apartment. I knew it would be a matter of hours. Williams' son and a friend were there, and they all got talking, on the dullest subject in the world, prohibition, — these brilliant men! And then there was another cocktail. They all wanted to go to the Coffee House for lunch where they have a table d'hote of three courses. And the talk even there was still of prohibition. I got back to the office at 3.30 and then found a man waiting to see me. A ruined afternoon! I had accomplished a great deal in the morning though, and anyhow, it had to be.

Your second letter to Zippy came tonight, and a very good one it was, but short. That's the only fault with your letters. Bopa was delighted with his. He sent it right off to Aunt Jenny. We never saw it at all. It pleased him so much that I hope you may have written him another.

The surprising good weather holds. Does it mean a wet spring? The feel of spring is in the air tonight, and it's warmer than we've had it; but the ground and the trees are as wintry as in December.

March 9th

Now it's all more wintry than in most Decembers. — Our first real snow storm, and such a driving fine snow that the commuters were all talking about blizzards in March. Snow is banked up against the steps and the storm door, and the wind is rushing across the country. I got snow in my shoes in walking up the hill from the station. It began to fall at nine, in large, damp flakes; but it grew colder and the flakes became small, dry and stinging.

Janey is truly better, and Nance is no worse. Jane has been so good, I bought her a *David Copperfield* with colored pictures and wrote in it: —

To
Jane Morton Perkins

In appreciation of
Her Courage, her Patience, and her
fine consideration of others during the
long nights and days of whooping cough

From her father
March 9th 1928

We've been reading *Henry Esmond* on the sofa on the side of the room. We're just about halfway through, and the children love it, especially Zippy. I went in to her last night to tuck her in and she half woke up and groped over me with her hands and said "Who are you? Who are you?" I said "Why Zippy, don't you know me?" And she said, "O Yes, *Uncle* Max."

I had a long letter from Helen Evarts from Saranac. She's very much better; — can even get up for a little. It was a spirited, cheerful letter to thank me for the books and magazines I'd sent her.

Mother is by the fire reading *Vogue*, — whatever she can find to read in it is beyond me! Peg, in pajamas, just came down to say Nance was crying. Cold! So everyone rushed to her, and she most ungracious, and shut the window and turned on the heater, and Mother rocked her and sang to her, and I warmed her bed with an electric lamp a man gave me, the boxing man. And now she says she's too hot!

I'll write no more darling. Maybe this letter will not reach you anyhow; but if it does it will be on the day you sail for home.

Your loving daddy
Maxwell E. Perkins

That trip was the beginning of the end, as my father must have known, even as he gently encouraged me to take the big step into the world alone. The following year I went away to school; Zippy followed, then Peg—our family unit was broken, as it had to be.

It was at this time, too, that Thomas Wolfe began to absorb more and more of his time and energy, Tom, who was later to write a book called, You Can't Go Home Again.